A GUIDEBOOK TO CONTEMPORARY ARCHITECTURE IN VANCOUVER

A GUIDEBOOK TO CONTEMPORARY ARCHITECTURE IN VANCOUVER

CHRIS MACDONALD
IN COLLABORATION WITH
VERONICA GILLIES

WITH ESSAYS BY
ADELE WEDER
MATTHEW SOULES

SERIES EDITORS
NANCY DUNTON
HELEN MALKIN

DOUGLAS & McINTYRE
D&M PUBLISHERS INC.
VANCOUVER/TORONTO/BERKELEY

Douglas & McIntyre
An imprint of D&M Publishers Inc.
2323 Quebec Street, Suite 201
Vancouver BC Canada V5T 4S7
www.douglas-mcintyre.com

Library and Archives Canada
Cataloguing in Publication

Macdonald, Christopher, 1953–
 A guidebook to contemporary architecture in Vancouver / Christopher Macdonald.

Includes index.
ISBN 978-1-55365-445-2

 1. Architecture—British Columbia—Vancouver—Guidebooks.
2. Vancouver (B.C.)—Buildings, structures, etc.—Guidebooks.
I. Title.

NA747.V3M33 2010
720.9711'3309051   C2009-905946-0

Printed and bound in China by C & C Offset Printing Co., Ltd.
Printed on acid-free paper
Distributed in the U.S. by Publishers Group West

Texts: Chris Macdonald
Editing: Jana Tyner, Heather Maxwell
Series Editors: Nancy Dunton and Helen Malkin
Research and Cartography: Heather Maxwell

Book Design: George Vaitkunas
Photography on cover and pages 2, 8 and 178: Gavin Mackenzie

The Royal Architectural   L'Institut royal
Institute of Canada   d'architecture du Canada

The authors gratefully acknowledge the financial support of the Royal Architectural Institute of Canada.

Special thanks to Vancouver architects Peeroj Thakre, Brian Billingsley, Clinton Cuddington and Gair Williamson for their thoughtful contributions to the guidebook selection process.

Additional thanks go to the author's family, friends and colleagues for their thoughtful comments and unflagging support.

Canada Council   Conseil des Arts
for the Arts   du Canada

The publisher gratefully acknowledges the financial support of the Canada Council for the Arts, the British Columbia Arts Council, the Province of British Columbia through the Book Publishing Tax Credit and the Government of Canada through the Book Publishing Industry Development Program (BPIDP) for its publishing activities.

This guidebook is dedicated to the memory of Arthur Erickson. In his distinguished designs for Vancouver he has taught all of us much about architecture, and much about what it might mean to be contemporary.

MAY 26 2010

CONTENTS

PREFACE

Why this book?

This guidebook is intended as a companion volume to similar introductions to the contemporary architecture of Montreal and Toronto. Each city has very different settlement histories and for each, architecture's role in portraying cultural forces remains distinct. Perhaps most obviously, Vancouver does not possess a significant stock of historic buildings, and its already modest industrial base has largely been made redundant during the post-war era. As a consequence, Vancouver presents an urban character that is vigorously contemporary.

The past twenty years have seen a period of unprecedented population growth accompanied by an extraordinary volume of new construction. Constrained by the city's geography and cultivated by forceful public policy, this construction is revealed most vividly in the dense aggregation of the downtown peninsula, while evident to varying degrees across the entire Lower Mainland landscape. This guide presents a selection of accomplished buildings, landscapes and precincts representing the varied interests that have shaped the emerging city.

Why these buildings?

A first principle in selecting projects for inclusion in the guide was simply a high level of design accomplishment, as acknowledged by the awards and reviews given by professional peers and critics. This alone, however, did not ensure inclusion and the degree to which projects served to exemplify significant design and cultural practices evident in Vancouver at this time, was also considered. The manner in which the City of Vancouver promotes public works through negotiated planning agreements is, for instance, a common theme that frames many of the entries. Similarly, the emergence of denser urban typologies in Vancouver's neighbouring municipalities is acknowledged in a number of projects.

As a rule, interiors and private homes have been excluded from the project selection. In the case of interiors, often-rapid alterations discourage their inclusion, although key exceptions have been made where the interior demonstrates significant urban principles. Particular effort has been made throughout the guide to bring attention to projects that contribute a common, public dimension to the city.

It is of note that a number of entries highlight building ensembles or urban precincts. This is not to undermine the accomplishments of individual buildings, but rather to point to the significance of Vancouver's broader, collective enterprise. To fashion a new metropolis at such a fast pace encourages an almost improvisational mode of practice, and has often resulted in the art of planning achieving a clarity more vivid than that of architecture *per se*. This is especially true in the large tracts of industrial lands recently developed that have proven to be so critical in defining Vancouver's contemporary identity.

Vancouver's West Coast pedigree is apparent in the pervasive enthusiasm for exacting environmental performance for every scale of design. From regional planning principles through to a whole variety of innovations in natural building systems, the projects exude a desire to push conventional construction and settlement practices towards new standards of energy use, material resolution and social responsibility. The alliance of this desire with public agency is a defining attribute of contemporary practice and is evident in virtually every project surveyed.

Bearing in mind both local and visiting enthusiasts, we have also made every effort to include projects that lie beyond the realm of 'the usual suspects'. No doubt, projects of merit have escaped our scrutiny and projects included may provoke skeptics. This collection of recent buildings and landscapes is intended to encourage a curious eye to look at those projects that did not find their way into the guide as well – to observe and consider the remarkable experiment in urban life and architecture called Vancouver.

Why this time period?

Working from a designated point of departure in 1990 through to the guide's publication neatly brackets the collection of projects between the important civic spectacles of the 1986 World Exposition and the 2010 Winter Olympics. The hosting of the 1986 Exposition provided an important stimulus to local design practices as well as promoting a new-found sense of confidence and critical self-awareness. Indeed many current architectural practices in Vancouver were forged at this time. The consequence of the Exposition site's subsequent redevelopment in shifting the scale and ambition of city making cannot be overstated.

Further, the process of planning and redeveloping the Concord Pacific site occurred in parallel with an important initiative to envision the future of the entire Lower Mainland. The planning strategy outlined in the policy document *'Creating Our Future'* of 1990 effectively set into place the region's vision for addressing issues of environmental health, growth management and transportation issues. This would in turn form the basis for the *'Livable Region Strategic Plan'*, adopted by the Greater Vancouver Regional District in 1996, a policy document that continues to inform local strategic planning. The pattern of transportation infrastructure, the desire to augment residential use in Vancouver's downtown core and increase density elsewhere, the logic of varied urban centres located throughout the region: all of these key concerns were identified and brought forward into various instruments of public policy at this time.

Who was this book written for?

Vancouver's reputation as a place for provocative urban experiment and accomplished architectural design draws a steady flow of design professionals from around the globe, and certainly the guidebook is intended for them. In its array of projects the guide is, we hope, an informative and stimulating companion for other visitors and especially for Vancouver citizens. The sublime natural surroundings will continue to draw attention, yet the emerging city shows signs of complexity and accomplishment that also invite curious investigation.

HOW TO USE THIS BOOK

This guidebook serves as an introduction to Vancouver's contemporary urban environment and to a wide variety of significant buildings and neighbourhoods. The projects have been chosen to be enjoyed, but also to stimulate. Consider the guide as both invitation and companion. Apart from its primary role to identify recent projects of significance, the commentary also aims to draw attention to qualities of the work that might otherwise escape notice – that is, to provide emphasis alongside context.

Buildings and places in this book are to varying degrees accessible by public transportation. Checking on timing and frequency of service of bus and skytrain systems is always advisable, at www.translink.ca. Projects included are also to varying degrees accessible to the public, and every attempt has been made to be clear about access to buildings (websites for further information have been included). Respect for privacy has been, and we believe should remain, paramount.

Projects to see are grouped according to local neighbourhoods. A short text about each gives a sense of the urban context, but there is, of course, much more to see and explore. The dispersed settlement pattern that exists beyond Vancouver's central downtown results in several projects that appear geographically isolated, yet the discovery of the urban environs of each of these will certainly offer its own satisfaction.

Maps of the neighbourhoods are oriented to the north – in Vancouver's case this means towards the mountains – and have adopted a consistent scale wherever possible. Significant buildings adjacent to the selected projects are also indicated in order to assist with local orientation.

Images of projects are typically but not exclusively those selected by the projects' architects themselves to present their work, and indicate the condition of the buildings at the time of completion. We are endlessly grateful to the architects, designers and photographers who responded to our requests for drawings and images. In every respect, this guide could not exist without their generous support.

Architects are identified by the name of the firm at the time of project completion, as are clients and professional collaborators. Indexes at the end of the guide are organized by building, by building type and by firm to facilitate cross-referencing.

To observe the city's architecture is to enter into the optimistic vision of its planners and designers and so to engage in the work-in-progress that is Vancouver. The city's sense of *becoming* can at times be palpable – an unusual experience in the face of architecture's qualities of stability and endurance.

Above all, Vancouver's evocation of process and invention invites our imaginations to speculate about the future. Enter and enjoy!

AN URBAN COLLECTIVE
ADELE WEDER

On August 7, 1971, officers on horseback charged into a crowd in Gastown, the original downtown core of Vancouver, and swung their batons at the thousand people who had gathered or wandered there to protest marijuana laws and the nefarious police tactics used to enforce them. At the intersection of Abbott and Cordova, marchers and onlookers were beaten or hauled into paddywagons and the public gathering soon transformed into what became known as the Gastown Riot, one of the most notorious brawls in the city's history. In the years that followed, the neighbourhood withered, its zoning geared towards the tawdry tourist outlets that would long dominate it, its days as a gathering site all but over.

Making architecture is, at its core, a political action. Implicit in the design approach is the decision to encourage or thwart public gatherings, nurture or displace the poor, ignite or asphyxiate streetlife, rabble-rouse or calm the streets for paying visitors. At first glance, the shiny newness of central Vancouver suggests a manifesto of clarity and order, a divergence from the fiery social consciousness of decades past. Underlying these images of finesse and resolve, however, are backstories of complex negotiations between public and private interests whose endgame is the greater public good. With increased density allowance as the currency, the resulting deals have spawned an unprecedented array of community centres, daycares, parks, public art and social housing.

As with many other instances described in this guide, Gastown's current robust and widely inclusive revival owes much to City Hall – the very institution that had sanctioned the police bullying and subsequent neighbourhood stagnation in the first place. The most conspicuous participant in this revival is Woodward's, an inventive reconstruction of the old department store into a fusion of slick condo tower, social housing, art school and community centre. The public-good aspect of the project – restoration of certain heritage components and rental units for lower-income residents – has only been possible through density bonusing, which afforded the developer the right to build higher and tighter, in exchange for embedding inclusivity into the complex.

Vancouver had suffered from architectural indifference and a dearth of public space long before the Gastown melee. Whether commercial or domestic, the early colonial-flavoured architecture did not lend itself to generating a public realm. Stanley Park and the waterfront became the dominant public amenity largely by default. Lacking centrifugal force and architectural frontage, the seawall is more promenade than piazza, with its linear circulation that resists spontaneous interaction. It is a fine space for exercising, or for watching a running spool of human faces. It is not the kind of space that is conducive to either quiet contemplation or expressions of civic discontent. Following Vancouver's benchmark hosting of a World Exposition in 1986, a new wave of collective urban consciousness emerged. As the idealism and power of individual clients and their architects waned, the impetus for creating new public spaces rose up from the same development forces that in the past often threatened to destroy the public inheritance. Moated by water and mountain, and an agricultural land reserve, the city quite simply had run out of land to build on.

With developers now dependent on the grace of City Hall to build up and inward, rather than ever outward, the City Hall now had a newly powerful tool-kit of zoning policies. Henceforth, citizens at large would have an ownership stake in the city skyline and vista, a stake to which the financier of a bulky office tower would now defer. The belief in the collective ownership of the city's dramatic natural vista translated into the 1989 mandating of 'view corridors', zoning which preserved glimpses of mountains and oceans for wayfarers in the centre of the city. So saturated is the architectural buildup in the city centre that, in Vancouver, the common meaning of 'corridor' is not the hallway inside a building, but the ever-more-rare lane of visual space that remains outside of it.

The complement to view-corridor policy evolved into the wholesale acceptance of the density bonus transfer system in the 1990s. The basic premise was to proffer the right to build higher and denser than the zoning book allowed, if in exchange the developers would bankroll a park, heritage restoration, community centre, social housing or other public project. Parks and outdoor sculpture and heritage restoration began to flourish as a by-product of development. The process challenged the notion that park space, art galleries, and community centres were a frill and redefined them an essential component of a city. Developers would henceforth be expected as a matter of civic responsibility to partner with the city in order to enhance, rather than merely augment, the built environment.

The legacy of this last stage of collective conscious contributes much to the content of this book. Woodward's, the Electra Building retrofit, the Wall and Shangri-La towers, GRANtable, Coal Harbour and the Contemporary Art Gallery are all examples of architecture that has either been a donor or beneficiary of the density bonusing mechanism. What this policy tool-kit allows is the creation of an architecture that finds a path around the ruthlessness and indifference of the marketplace. That midcentury masterpiece, the former B.C. Electric headquarters, could find new life only as a residential tower. But its spacious hallways and elegant tile mosaic and meticulous retrofitting would have been doomed within an indifferent marketplace in which condominium units are bought and sold like stock options.

The architectural stock of Vancouver has made many of its residents – and also a good number of faraway investors - desperately rich, so much so that $18-million has become a kind of signifier price for a tower's penthouse, the masthead that brands it as a building worth buying into. At the new Shangri-La tower, unlike Woodward's and Coal Harbour, there are no on-site amenities for the low-income; its ground floor is dominated by a boutique food store while its restaurant is a five-star dining and paying experience. Shangri-La does, however, contribute to the public realm in major ways: aesthetically (it raises the bar for the otherwise-banal glass towers in the vicinity); financially (its developer 'bought' the density by paying for heritage restoration elsewhere); culturally (by providing an ancillary public sculpture court for the Vancouver Art Gallery); and environmentally (through the cultivation of a compact onsite forestland to offset carbon deficits). The game of trades and rewards extends beyond the material fact of building to encompass the full spectrum of human activity.

Abbott and Cordova, 7 August 1971 by Stan Douglas

Not far from this gleaming copse of downtown towers is its urban counterpoint, the Downtown Eastside. Once the affluent city centre, this century-old neighbourhood has devolved into one of the most impoverished and troubled communities in the country, but one with fierce local pride and sense of ownership. Architecturally ambitious social housing – Bruce Eriksen Place, Lore Krill Housing Co-Operative, the Portland Hotel Society, and others – convey a message that housing remains for all of us a crucial program: that local residents are also full citizens. And the message is conveyed not only directly to the surrounding citizens but also through the experience of the city to more cosseted, comfortable neighbourhoods.

Woodward's itself is now a bulwark against the gentrification or touristification juggernaut, hard-wired as it is to house a variety of socio-demographic categories. Beyond the complex array of building uses, the developer also bankrolled the project's centrepiece installation: an eight-by-thirteen-metre mural by renowned Vancouver artist Stan Douglas. Composed from over 50 separate photographs that have been enlarged and superimposed, the tableau depicts frantic young protesters being harassed and beaten by baton-wielding cops, with the old Woodward building in the background. It's the Gastown Riot, re-imagined, and anyone can view it by walking into the publicly accessible foyer. Here the historical record is rendered as carefully framed urban scenery for a new generation. The mural's terse geographic title, *Abbott & Cordova, 7 August 1971*, is more appropriate and more forgiving than entitling it *The Gastown Riot*. By honouring the intersection with its title, it suggests that while ideologies and rhetoric and city-hall regimes inevitably come and go, our city streets – and our will to inhabit them – will last a much longer time.

DOWNTOWN CENTRAL

Vancouver's downtown precinct is defined most vividly by its geography. An elongated peninsula terminating to the west in Stanley Park, its proximity to the shoreline contributes to the image and identity of the city. While still dominated by office and commercial functions, Vancouver's downtown core has been overlaid by residential buildings over the past generation, largely in the form of point-block towers straddling some form of low-rise podium. Their success in attracting residents to the area has been such that recent conversions of existing commercial structures into condominiums suggests a future in which the traditional downtown employment base might be eroded by the transformation of the city centre into a kind of residential resort.

The architectural resolution of these new towers is less convincing than their planning, although the image of the aggregation is striking. The City has been resolute in providing social and cultural amenities to accompany the redevelopment, and it is there that much of the centre's design interest resides. It should be noted that in the negotiated delivery of such ameni- ties in return for increased built density, not only are the services provided but public awareness of the City's role of the in such transactions is also enhanced. The prevailing enthusiasm for the ethos of 'Vancouverism' is, in this context, as much an indication of pride in active, progressive gover- nance as it is in the planning outcomes themselves.

CONTEMPORARY ART GALLERY

Crisply detailed gallery and support spaces provide a refreshing street-level cultural presence near the city's commercial core. Of the numerous public amenities derived from development density agreements with the City, the CAG remains exemplary. Granted a raw 'shell' space by the developer – contingent upon the CAG establishing endowment funds to cover ongoing operating costs – the project provides positive demonstration of the potential finesse that can be exacted through the actions of tenant building improvements. This a welcome reminder in a city of generally undistinguished interior environments.

Architect	**Stantec Architecture Ltd., Martin Lewis + nlm Architect**
Client	**Contemporary Art Gallery**
Completed	**2001**
Address	**555 Nelson Street**
Transit	**Yaletown-Roundhouse**
Access	**free admission with suggested donation, www.contemporaryartgallery.ca**

DOWNTOWN CENTRAL

LIBRARY SQUARE

The central facility for the Vancouver Public Library was the result of an exceptionally rare competition process in which both expert and public opinion was included in the adjudication process. An early instance of city-block scaled mixed-use development, the dominant oval figure of the library is augmented with a federal office tower, retail and service facilities. An elliptical enclosed galleria deflects pedestrian flow from the adjacent street frontages, concluding in largely undifferentiated but usefully tiered external plazas. The expanded facility was timed with near-perfect anticipation of the burgeoning downtown residential population and the project is extremely popular. Regular public events scheduled by an ambitious and responsible civic institution certainly contribute to the project's success – this despite an exterior surface that is ungenerous and isolated from the primary commercial and public occasions of the city. The exterior elevations bereft of the two primary galleria entries remain dismal.

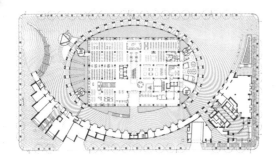

Architect	**Moshe Safdie Associates Ltd., DA Architects + Planners**
Landscape	**Cornelia Hahn Oberlander**
Client	**City of Vancouver**
Completed	**1995**
Address	**350 West Georgia Street**
Transit	**Granville, Vancouver City Centre, Stadium**
Access	**public, www.vpl.vancouver.bc.ca**

DOWNTOWN CENTRAL

THE ELECTRA

The original design was historically key in declaring Vancouver's embrace of not only a progressive urban agenda, but of the local capacity to render that ambition with a highly accomplished modern architecture. The renovation of commercial spaces and their re-casting as condominium units is emblematic of the success in attracting residents to the downtown core over the past two decades.

Equally important is the meticulous renewal of the original curtain wall in order to meet contemporary building code and envelope performance expectations. In a city as young as Vancouver debates around heritage preservation can all too easily ignore the importance of valuing even very recent works of merit. The original decorative tile work by early modern artist B.C. Binning speaks to the comprehensive ambitions of the modern project and continues to project a sense of bright optimism into the city fabric.

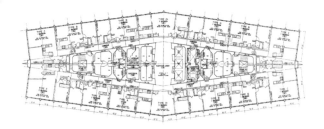

Architect	**Merrick Architecture-Borowski Lintott Sakumoto Fligg Ltd.**
Client	**Prime Tower Limited, Harrowston Developments Corporation**
Completed	**1995**
Address	**970 Burrard Street, 989 Nelson Street**
Transit	**Burrard, Vancouver City Centre**
Access	**exterior only, ground level commercial**

DOWNTOWN CENTRAL

ONE WALL CENTRE

A combination of hotel and residential accommodation, One Wall Centre briefly held the position as tallest structure in Vancouver and garnered headlines for the controversy surrounding its glazed exterior. Disagreement during construction regarding the chosen colour and opacity of the glass façade led to a compromise decision in which a more transparent panel was installed on the upper third of the building, leading to its ultimate and curious two-tone appearance.

The transfer of density from several historic structures elsewhere in the downtown core sanctioned the additional building height. The tower's modest floor-plate and oval configuration do much in creating a striking profile amidst the skyline of downtown Vancouver. They also inadvertently inspire a degree of ingenuity in the sensible organization of hotel suites and condominium layouts – a latter day instance of function following form after all.

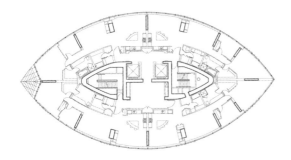

Architect	**Busby Perkins+Will**
Structure	**Glotman Simpson Consulting Engineers**
Landscape	**Phillips Farevaag Smallenberg**
Client	**Wall Financial Corporation**
Completed	**2001**
Address	**1001 Hornby Street**
Transit	**Burrard, Vancouver City Centre**
Access	**lobby only**

SCOTIABANK DANCE CENTRE

As is often the case in Vancouver, the collage of contemporary necessity and historic legacy is reduced to the preservation of an historic façade, behind which an entirely new programme of use is constructed. While in certain instances – market housing renovations in Gastown, for instance – this tactic serves to actively undermine the clarity of the contemporary design, in this instance the preservation of the neoclassical elevation simply restricts the capacity to express the vitality of the Dance Centre interior. In so doing, the retention of the façade – a former bank – suggests a degree of institutional *gravitas* that is inconsistent with the actual demeanor of the building's occupant.

In a city possessing a remarkably modest historic building legacy, the effort to retain significant material artifacts must of course be taken seriously. In this instance – notwithstanding the imaginative new construction – the consequence of this well-meaning instinct verges on parody.

Architect	**Stantec Architecture Ltd., in collaboration with Arthur Erickson**
Client	**Dance Foundation, Scotiabank Dance Theatre**
Completed	**2000**
Address	**677 Davie Street**
Transit	**Yaletown-Roundhouse**
Access	**lobby only**

GRANtable

Produced as a component of the City's ongoing 'Art in Public Places' project, this overscaled installation of urban furniture takes its cue from the grand rooms of neoclassical architecture. The use of the 66 foot long table ranges from being an empty piece of heroic sculpture to providing a site for large community picnics. In either case, it provides a Lilliputian scene for the many surrounding condominium dwellers to view from above. The work invites speculation on the decorum of City parks more generally and brings an encouraging sense of play into the urban condition.

Architect	**Pechet and Robb Art and Architecture Ltd.**
Structure	**JM Engineering**
Client	**City of Vancouver, Board of Parks and Recreation**
Completed	**1998**
Address	**801 Beach Avenue (Mae and Lorne Brown Park)**
Transit	**Yaletown-Roundhouse**
Access	**public**

Waterfront

Waterfront

CRAB Park
at Portside

Richards

Water

Gastown

Trounce Alley

Inform
Interiors

Salt
Tasting
Room
& Salt
Cellar

Alexander

Powell

W Cordova

E Cordova

Homer

Hamilton

Victoria
Square

Woodward's
Redevelopment

W Hastings

E Hastings

Bruce
Eriksen
Place

VanCity
Place for
Youth

Cambie

Portland
Hotel

33 West
Pender

W Pender

E Pender

Chinatown

← page 20

Beatty

Abbott

Taylor

Carrall

Columbia

Main

Strathcona

Stadium

Keefer

E Georgia

Citadel Parade

Dunsmuir Viaduct

Andy
Livingstone
Park

Union

Georgia Viaduct

Expo Blvd

Pacific Blvd

Prior

Milross

National

Quebec

Main

Station

Creekside
Park

Main

0   100 metres

1 minute to walk

DOWNTOWN EAST SIDE

To the east of downtown's commercial core lies the precinct initially settled and retaining the largest assemblage of historic building fabric in Vancouver. As retail and office uses migrated westward and the car replaced the streetcar as the prevalent means of transportation, the area suffered from both physical and social neglect. In particular, the traditional reliance on seasonal resource-based employment for an itinerant work force was challenged by changes in technology, contributing to significant unemployment in the area.

Often characterized as 'the poorest postal code in Canada', the Downtown Eastside and adjacent neighbourhoods of Gastown, historic Chinatown and Strathcona present a complex and challenging urban environment unlike any other precinct in Vancouver. Undergoing various forms of renewal, gentrification and decline – all simultaneously – the precinct can at times be viewed as evidence of the ultimate limitation of architecture to serve as an agent for social progress and change.

Efforts to redevelop buildings in the area are often constrained by the relatively small width of the original single building street frontage of twenty-five feet. Particularly in Chinatown, where smallholdings may also be accompanied by complex ownership, the result can be a kind of inertia that only aggravates the physical decline of the structures. This being said, the area includes a number of accomplished infill projects that preserve much of the scale and detail of the historic fabric.

VANCITY PLACE FOR YOUTH

While modern architecture's intervention in historic urban settings has often resulted in uneasy juxtapositions, this modest social housing infill project provides an exemplary lesson in contextual deference. The matter-of-fact overall composition is resolved with a thoughtful combination of massing and attention to material detail while the new construction literally embraces a renovated historic structure next door. Street-level retail space below the dense aggregation of housing units helps to manage pedestrian scale and continuity. An evident lack of maintenance now detracts from the initial confidence of the street elevation, while the commercial space at grade has yet to find a stable tenancy – evidence of the limits of design in the resolution of what are hugely complex social dynamics.

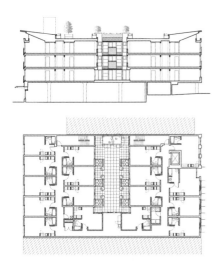

Architect	**Nigel Baldwin Architects**
Client	**VanCity Enterprises Ltd.**
Completed	**1997**
Address	**326 West Pender Street**
Transit	**Stadium, Waterfront**
Access	**exterior only**

33 WEST PENDER

While the development of renovated existing structures and modestly scaled social housing has provided the most durable renewal of downtown Vancouver's historic centre, new private sector housing infill projects have also played a role. This particular instance provides considerably higher density rendered with a distinctly contemporary expressive idiom, yet also strives to produce a scale and degree of surface texture that is sympathetic to its neighbours.

Most successful in acknowledging the decorum of the street elevation, the magnitude of increase in density and building volume is revealed more assertively to the lane behind.

Architect	**Acton Ostry Architects**
Structure	**Glotman Simpson Consulting Engineers**
Client	**Georgia Laine Developments Ltd.**
Completed	**2009**
Address	**33 West Pender Street**
Transit	**Stadium, Waterfront**
Access	**exterior only**

BRUCE ERICKSEN PLACE

In a city only recently constructed and often of fragile material substance, the question of how to perpetuate collective social history is challenging. In the context of this project for social housing, the challenge is amplified since the history being recalled is devoted not to those who exercised authority over the construction of the city, but rather to those who interceded in the human dimension of its daily life. The naming of streets, public parks and in this instance a building providing social housing all contribute to projecting some sense of common history forward – with architecture's role in this enterprise oftentimes ambiguously positioned.

This project builds with generosity, presenting a sense of dignity towards the realm of the street that shelters the daily communion of its inhabitants. It also works creatively within what otherwise might become paternal agencies of public art provisions and governing space standards to ensure that significant past contributions to the community are remembered.

Architect **Henriquez Partners Architects**
Client **Main & Hastings Housing Society**
Completed **1995**
Address **380 Main Street**
Transit **Stadium, Waterfront**
Access **private**

PORTLAND HOTEL

The Portland Hotel Society provides and manages housing for those on the very threshold of homelessness. Here, their mission is expressed in distinctive and suitably robust metal cladding with a variegated street elevation that hints at the diminutive scale of the rooms within. The street level café has proven to be a durable tenant, making a positive contribution to the texture and cadence of the pedestrian realm. To the rear of the building, care has been taken to preserve a protected courtyard garden accessible to tenants.

Architect	**Nick Milkovich Architects Inc. with Arthur Erickson**
Structure	**C.Y. Loh & Associates Ltd.**
Landscape	**Cornelia Hahn Oberlander**
Client	**Portland Hotel Society**
Completed	**1999**
Address	**20 West Hastings Street**
Transit	**Stadium, Waterfront**
Access	**exterior and café**

WOODWARD'S REDEVELOPMENT

This extensive redevelopment involves a mix of market and non-market housing units, anchor food and drugstore, retail, urban green space, public plaza, federal and civic offices, a daycare and a significant addition to the downtown campus of Simon Fraser University. The retained heritage portion of the complex is restored to contain a suite of non-profit community spaces. Once a thriving department store, the site's renewal brings with it the promise of bringing a diverse and vibrant array of programmes back to the neighbourhood. Beyond its own internal logic, the project's unprecedented density presents a vivid juxtaposition of scale to its historic surroundings.

The result of a lengthy two-stage competition and substantial subsequent community engagement, the project resurrects a once vital site in the midst of an economically challenged community. The strategy of emphasizing the public role of the internal courtyard rather than supporting existing streetscapes is bold, and its success will ultimately be critical in determining the full measure of accomplishment in urban terms.

The project integrates fragments of the existing 1908 building and further references the surroundings' material heritage in its application of metal screens and lower level brickwork. The adjacent Lore Krill Housing Cooperative building anticipates the more extensive Woodward's site in material character and further contributes to the diverse housing types in this precinct. Planted exterior facades and roofs declare the project's commitment to sustainability at an expansive urban scale.

Architect	**Henriquez Partners Architects**
Community Liaison	**Jim Green**
Structure	**Glotman Simpson Consulting Engineers**
Client	**Westbank Projects & Peterson Investment Group**
Completed	**2010**
Address	**100 West Cordova**
Transit	**Stadium, Waterfront**
Access	**public, private residential**

INFORM INTERIORS

This retail development represents a substantial renovation and addition to an existing heritage building. Whereas common practice in Gastown development retains only the street elevation – quite literally one brick thick – here, significant aspects of the original structure are maintained. Wooden floors are pressed into service as permanent formwork for new concrete floors, which stabilize the front elevation while bearing on new concrete supports that mark the structural bays of the original wood columns.

The thoughtfully detailed interior is focused on a generously dimensioned staircase that rises from basement to roof, crowned by a substantial skylight. Virtually unique in Vancouver, the publicly accessible rooftop offers exceptional views of the neighbourhood and North Shore mountains alongside a tantalizing glimpse of the immense potential for such roof-scapes to enrich the urban experience. Extravagant interior and furnishings notwithstanding, the pleasure of the rooftop is not to be missed.

Architect	**Busby Perkins+Will**
Interior Design	**Omer Arbel and Niels Bendtsen**
Client	**50 Water Street Holdings / Blood Alley Holdings**
Completed	**2006**
Address	**50 Water Street**
Transit	**Stadium, Waterfront**
Access	**business hours**

SALT TASTING ROOM & SALT CELLAR

A modest ground level and basement renovation of an existing Gastown structure, this restaurant gains much of its interest in pioneering the possibility of directly accessing commercial activities from Vancouver's downtown service lanes. The acute juxtaposition of social milieus that results from such an experiment is vivid, and the artfully fashioned contemporary bay window overlooking the alley confronts the juxtaposition with confidence. Inside, the installation studiously avoids the excesses of unbridled gentrification, resulting in un-fussy yet carefully executed gathering places.

Architect	**Busby Perkins+Will**
Interiors	**Scott Hawthorn, Sean Heather,**
	Gair Williamson Architects
Client	**Blood Alley Holdings**
Completed	**2006**
Address	**45 Blood Alley**
Transit	**Stadium, Waterfront**
Access	**business hours**

Waterfront Station 2 blocks

Canada Place

Amenity Landscapes

Vancouver Convention Centre West

Habour Green Park

Coal Harbour Community Centre

W Cordova

W Hastings

Dunsmuir

W Pender

Melville

Burrard

Nicola

Broughton

Jervis

Bute

Thurlow

Burrard

Hornby

Howe

W Georgia

Alberni

Shangri-La Vancouver

← page 62

page 20

Robson

Haro

Barclay Heritage Square

Barclay

Smithe

Nelson

Comox

Nelson Park

Helmcken

Pendrell

St. Paul's Hospital

Mole Hill Housing

0   100 metres

1 minute to walk

Davie

DOWNTOWN WEST SIDE

On the west side of downtown, the commercial intensity of Robson Street and the more ceremonial presence of West Georgia anchor an area of diverse building type and imagery. The redevelopment of the industrial land known as Coal Harbour reconnected this precinct to the waterfront, extending the seawall promenade while creating a series of open spaces that more graciously conclude the north-south streetscapes. The varied scales of development are especially conspicuous in this part of Vancouver, with several generations of civic imagination literally juxtaposed one with another.

Amidst the architectural ambitions evident, it is interesting to compare the material opulence of the Shangri-La tower with the original 1969 MacMillan Bloedel headquarters designed by Arthur Erickson across Georgia Street – smoke and mirrors facing off with post-war Doric, as it were.

VANCOUVER CONVENTION CENTRE WEST

This major expansion of Vancouver's convention hosting capacity was constructed, in part, to serve as the International Broadcast Centre for the 2010 Olympic Winter Games. Something of the aura of spectacle remains in the form of both the building and the adjacent public plaza. As the city has added this new layer of construction onto its waterfront the scale of a new era has emerged, measured against the dimension and impetus of passing cruise ships as much as the activities of adjacent streets.

The project's sustainability goals are most evident in the vast expanse of green roof – particularly striking when viewed from further west along the sea wall pedestrian path. Less evident but curious is the creation of an artificial reef along the harbour flank of the building, visible at low tide. The positive engagement between building and plaza with the linear experience of the seawall has acquired public use even prior to the full implementation of the various functional programs.

Architect	**LMN Architects, DA Architects + Planners, Musson Cattell Mackey Partnership**
Structure	**Glotman Simpson Consulting Engineers**
Landscape	**PWL Partnership Landscape Architects Inc.**
Client	**PavCo (BC Pavilion Corp.)**
Completed	**2009**
Address	**1055 Canada Place**
Transit	**Burrard, Waterfront**
Access	**exterior, interior lobby**

COAL HARBOUR COMMUNITY CENTRE

The construction of significant landscaped open spaces alongside the recent generation of downtown development is critical in creating the modernist imagery of towers set in a common, continuous garden. In the case of the Coal Harbour Community Centre, community facilities are literally subsumed within the new parkland, deferring to the virtues of visual openness and verdure.

The integration of the handsome and robust interiors with the surrounding landscape also serves the purpose of making a clear distinction between the territorial realm of private dwelling place and the collective landscape. While the community centre and its surrounding parkland owe their existence to Coal Harbour's condominium developments, the 'gated' condition of the towers remains explicit.

Architect **Henriquez Partners Architects**
Landscape **Philips Wuori Long Inc.**
Client **Marathon Developments Inc.**
Completed **2000**
Address **480 Broughton Street**
Transit **Burrard**
Access **public**

SHANGRI-LA VANCOUVER

The Living Shangri-La project serves as emblem of planning strategies that have privileged specific view corridors and designated sites capable of accommodating greater height in order to add visual interest to the city skyline. Currently the tallest structure in the city at 62 storeys, the project represents the extreme condition of substantial urban projects that cultivate mixed use and contribute public amenity as a precondition to their unprecedented density.

The Shangri-La combines a five-star hotel, 234 live-work units, 66 residential units complemented by ground level retail, grocery store and even a public sculpture garden for the Vancouver Art Gallery. As such, it offers a west side counterpoint to the Woodward's Redevelopment – interestingly both undertaken by the same development and marketing team. The project received a density transfer in return for the preservation of the adjacent heritage church – yet one more disparate element in a sometimes disorienting street level landscape. More successful is the attention paid to the tower's exterior, a lushly detailed curtain wall that offers visual texture to the landmark at a distance – particularly in late afternoon light – and yet is finely enough grained to forego excessive monumentality when experienced in closer proximity.

Architect	**James K.M. Cheng Architects**
Structure	**Jones Kwong Kishi,**
Landscape	**Phillips Farevaag Smallenberg**
Client	**KBK#11 Ventures Limited**
Completed	**2009**
Address	**1128 West Georgia Street**
Transit	**Burrard**
Access	**exterior, interior lobby**

AMENITY LANDSCAPES

While the encouraging carrot of *quid pro quo* is commonplace in planning authority negotiations elsewhere, in contemporary Vancouver high land values and the mandate for case-by-case density agreements throughout the downtown core have resulted in an aggregate of amenity landscapes larger than Manhattan's Central Park. The visual consequence of these cumulative actions is an urban landscape in central Vancouver that approximates early modernist conceptions of the city – the metropolitan imagery of high-rise towers held together by a ubiquitous *jardin anglais* of refined and apparently accessible landscape.

Evident throughout the downtown peninsula, projects on the western side contain some of the more flamboyant expressions of the genre. Water features abound, and the pervasive ambition to portray natural and native landscapes in the midst of urbanity is also remarkable. What lingers – perhaps more provocatively for the resident than the visitor – is the sense that this terrain is largely disengaged from the contours of everyday life. What remains is a landscape deeply imbedded in the perceived imagery of the city, yet curiously mute in contributing to any emerging urbanity.

Transit **Burrard**
Access **public**

MOLE HILL HOUSING

Situated in the middle of a high-density residential neighbourhood and an area of escalating investment property, this enclave of remaining timber-framed houses – latterly occupied as rooming houses – became a bellwether of attitude towards issues of preservation and urban character. The project transformed twenty-six of the heritage homes into affordable housing, but more importantly developed an urban strategy of expanding the virtues of informal laneway pedestrian spaces. At the same time, the structures were upgraded to accommodate contemporary green building techniques and energy efficient features. The laneways include shared community gardens, both subsidized and market rental housing and serve as an enduring witness to community accomplishment in the face of a very different development status quo.

Architect	**Hotson Bakker Boniface Haden, S.R. McEwen Associated Architects**
Heritage	**Donald Luxton & Associates Inc.**
Landscape	**Durante Kreuk Ltd.**
Client	**Mole Hill Community Housing Society, BC Housing, City of Vancouver**
Completed	**2003**
Address	**between Bute, Thurlow, Comox and Pendrell Streets**
Transit	**Burrard**
Access	**public grounds, private residential**

Stanley
Park

**Pacific
Canada
Pavilion**

Pipeline

Stanley Park Dr

Stanley Park
Causeway

N Lagoon

Devonian
Harbour
Park

Bayshore

W Georgia

Alberni

Robson

Haro

Barclay

Nelson

Lagoon

Stanley
Park

Park Lane

Chilco

Gilford

Denman

Comox

Bidwell

Cardero

Pendrell

The Eugenia
Beach

Davie

0   100 metres

1 minute to walk

WEST END

Vancouver's West End is an urban enclave unique in its combination of high population density with collective public amenity. With many of the early multi-family residential buildings occupying what had been single-family lots, the 1960s transformation of the neighbourhood emphasized small units with small building footprints, resulting in the curious and compelling streetscapes of mid-rise towers complete with front gardens. The continuous landscape that results contributes hugely to the quality of the precinct, providing a positive foreground to what is largely modest, background architecture.

PACIFIC CANADA PAVILION

This irregularly configured space draws together previously existing and disparate buildings and provides a potent sense of arrival and orientation for visitors to Vancouver's Aquarium. The dramatically daylit congregation area effectively contrasts with the sometimes disorienting experience of the display areas' low-level lighting. Distinguished by the propped beam-trusses of its roof structure, the experience is unsentimental in its reminiscence of the surrounding forest's light qualities. At the same time, the presence of a dramatically exposed marine exhibit anticipates the underwater sensation that characterizes many of the exhibits within. On its one exposed exterior elevation, the building provides a suitably delicate backdrop to the amphitheatre overlooking the dolphins and beluga whales.

Architect	**Bing Thom Architects**
Structure	**Fast + Epp Structural Engineers**
Client	**Vancouver Aquarium and Marine Science Centre**
Completed	**1999**
Address	**845 Avison Way**
Transit	**bus 19**
Access	**public, with paid admission**

THE EUGENIA

This 17-storey, 22-unit apartment tower brings a level of compositional care that is largely missing from the surrounding towers of the West End. Whether or not the observer is aware of the architect's design narrative – which draws literal reference to prior historical occupation of the site – the clarity of the resulting form and its confident execution distinguish the result.

While the expressive references – including ersatz ruins – are very direct, the reminder of times passed is remarkable in the context of Vancouver's general habits of building and as such not unwelcome. Most conspicuous is the solitary rooftop tree, signaling the height of the forest at the time Europeans first arrived on this coast. Million dollar views wrapped up in a timely history lesson.

Architect	**Henriquez Partners Architects**
Client	**Burrard International Holdings**
Completed	**1987**
Address	**1919 Beach Avenue**
Transit	**bus 6**
Access	*private*

FALSE CREEK / FAIRVIEW

The redevelopment of the industrial lands surrounding False Creek – located just south of the downtown peninsula – has proved a fertile ground for a host of variations in masterplanned urban design executed across substantial geographic areas. While this contemporary survey focuses on the Concord Pacific lands and the still emerging development of South East False Creek, the earlier parceling of residential projects on South West False Creek – adjacent to Granville Island – declares its own distinctive sense of how a new and thriving city might house itself.

Perhaps as significant as the residential enclaves themselves, there has been through the course of this redevelopment process a sustained project to provide continuous public access to the waterfront. To walk the perimeter of False Creek is certainly to observe a local history of urban design in Vancouver, but also to sense the vitality and variation in character that occurs along the length of the seaside promenade. From urbane corniche to faux 'natural' islands, past community centres, museums and public parkways, this inhabited edge of the city remains, without question, its extended cultural centre.

CONCORD PACIFIC PLACE

The decision to sell the entirety of the lands used for the 1986 Exposition as a single development property prompted a negotiated masterplanning that would result in the most significant single urban undertaking of its era. The scale of the project – 200 acres and 8000 residential units – and its central location allowed the City to ensure that a full array of programs and social intentions were realized alongside the predominant desire to bring market housing into the city centre. The 'tower and podium' format ensured that street frontages were created in the process, and public parkland, social housing and commercial and retail space completed the veritably utopian urban vision.

The aggregation of so many slender, largely glazed towers has come to serve as a defining image of Vancouver's recent prosperity and signal the city's own sense of accomplishment within a larger world stage of urban experience. Architecturally the projects almost to a fault defer to the diagram of urban design intent.

Design Team	**Baker McGarva Hart, Hulbert Group, Downs/Archambault, James K.M. Cheng, Davidson Yuen Simpson**
Client	**Concord Pacific Group**
Completed	**ongoing**
Address	**between Granville, Pacific Boulevard, Quebec and north side of False Creek**
Transit	**Yaletown-Roundhouse**
Access	**public, private residential**

SOUTH EAST FALSE CREEK

The final portion of the False Creek waterfront lands to be redeveloped was given an assertive jumpstart by including the first building projects as temporary sites for use during the 2010 Olympic Games. Current issues of sustainable building practice were highlighted throughout a lengthy planning process, as was the effort to ensure that sustainable urban design would mandate a diverse and inclusive spectrum of inhabitants and activities. Desire is also apparent to not simply replicate the pattern successfully described in the Concord Pacific Lands' development, but to seek a lower-rise, while equally populous configuration.

The visual density at street level is quite startling in comparison with prior constructions in the vicinity of False Creek, while the meticulously mannered landscape of the shoreline provides a new extreme in design aspiration for this public amenity. The conceit of 'Habitat Island' as a simulacrum of pre-existing native landscape is truly 'supernatural' in such a context.

Design Team	**Merrick Architecture-Borowski Lintott Sakumoto Fligg Limited, Gomberoff Bell Lyon Architects Group Inc., Lawrence Doyle Young & Wright Architects, Nick Milkovich Architects Inc. with Arthur Erickson, Robert Ciccozzi Architecture Inc, Walter Francl Architect Inc.**
Landscape	**Durante Kreuk Ltd., PWL Partnership Landscape Architects Inc.,**
Client	**City of Vancouver, Millennium Southeast False Creek Properties Ltd.**
Completed	**2009**
Address	**between Main, Cambie and south side of False Creek**
Transit	**Olympic Village, Main**
Access	**public, private residential**

FALSE CREEK / FAIRVIEW

BRITISH COLUMBIA CANCER RESEARCH CENTRE

The Cancer Research Centre contains facilities for the Genome Sequence Centre and amenities that include a theatre, library and food service. With its penthouse lounge and terrace, the Centre provides one of the very few occasions in which panoramic views of the city and its surroundings are revealed. In the midst of all of this public generosity the important business of six floors of laboratory are executed with modular rationality and lively expressive presence.

Not immediately evident is perhaps the ultimate measure of generosity – the provision of natural daylight in the interstitial service floors. The lower third of each of the grandly scaled circular windows actually delivers clerestory light to the array of mechanical and electrical systems that give flexible currency to the laboratory floors above and below. In its massing, material resolution and regard for the surrounding streetscape the building is unparalleled among the many medical facility buildings in this precinct of the city.

Architect **Henriquez Partners Architects, IBI Group**
Client **BC Cancer Foundation**
Completed **2004**
Address **675 West 10th Avenue**
Transit **Broadway-City Hall**
Access **public ground level**

BROADWAY / MAIN

As the downtown peninsula's sites for new development are transformed, pressure increases to allow greater population density in other areas of the city. The build-up of mixed-use projects along traditional transit corridors has proven to be a particularly effective strategy in absorbing density, while causing only modest disruption to settled neighbourhoods of single-family dwellings. The transformation of Broadway around Main and Kingsway begins to demonstrate the new sense of density in the precinct, and one can perceive a first glimpse of a distinctive urban ambience on the horizon.

STELLA

This mixed-use project marking the burgeoning intersection of Main and Kingsway exemplifies the emergence of new prototypes for dense accommodation beyond the central city core. The downtown habit of podium and tower is rendered with less attention to the scenography created by the podium's streetwall, here deftly accommodating an auto showroom that on its own would be perfectly at ease in any old suburban commercial strip.

The resolution of material detail distinguishes the project from comparable condominium projects, amplifying its astute urban attitude. In particular, the coloured glazing of end elevations offers a welcome light touch to the otherwise rather homely neighbourhood townscape. Gentrification of a sort, but played out with a clarity of vision that bodes well for the next cycle of more intense local development. The street level public landscape, unfortunately, only undermines the strengths of the project by projecting a sense of grudging concession rather than encouraging a positive contribution to its surroundings.

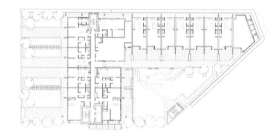

Architect **Acton Ostry Architects**
Structure **Glotman Simpson Consulting Engineers**
Client **350 Kingsway Development Ltd.**
Completed **2008**
Address **2770 Sophia Street**
Transit **Main + bus 3**
Access **public ground level, commercial space**

SUN 1

While the tower and podium format typical of recent development in the downtown core has come to personify Vancouver's new urbanism, the increase in population density in many existing residential neighbourhoods has adopted very different dwelling types. This particular example is thoughtful in its treatment of the exterior landscape spaces that become quite crucial to the collective pleasures of living at this density – a sort of bridging position between the isolated single family house and the metropolitan imagery of the tower type. The measured restraint of the exterior also speaks to a concern for promoting the virtues of a good neighbour.

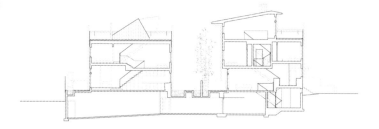

Architect	**BattersbyHowat,**
	Hancock Bruckner, Eng + Wright
Client	**Revolution Developments**
Completed	**2006**
Address	**3101 Prince Edward Street**
Transit	**Main + bus 3**
Access	**exterior only**

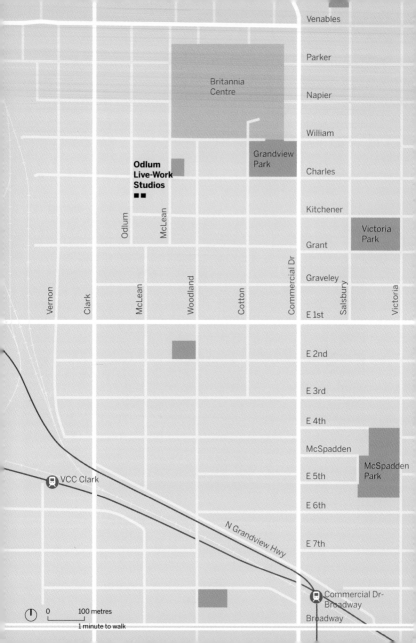

**Odlum
Live-Work
Studios**
■ ■

Venables

Parker

Napier

Britannia
Centre

William

Grandview
Park

Charles

Kitchener

Victoria
Park

Odlum

McLean

Grant

Graveley

Vernon

Clark

McLean

Woodland

Cotton

Commercial Dr

Salsbury

Victoria

E 1st

E 2nd

E 3rd

E 4th

McSpadden

McSpadden
Park

E 5th

E 6th

VCC Clark

N Grandview Hwy

E 7th

Commercial Dr-
Broadway

Broadway

0   100 metres

1 minute to walk

COMMERCIAL DRIVE

84 ODLUM LIVE-WORK STUDIOS

The area surrounding Commercial Drive supports a thriving commercial high-street with a diverse mixture of residential housing types and adjacent industrial use. As industry shifts to the city perimeter, coupled with the emergence of the 'knowledge economy', significant tracts of warehouse lands are under pressure to convert to residential uses. On the central and eastern extremes of Vancouver, in particular, effort has been made to maintain a productive employment base while acknowledging the ultimate necessity of redevelopment.

The creation of a live-work typology, initially intended to support artists and craft production, has become a new component of the urban landscape and brought a degree of nuance to traditional residential/commercial land use dichotomies. As a calculated antidote to gentrification-by-condominium the result is modest but not insignificant. Other examples of the genre may be seen in the area of Main Street and Second Avenue, further west from the Commercial Drive and Clark Avenue precinct.

ODLUM LIVE-WORK STUDIOS

Of the various purpose built 'live-work' projects in the vicinity, this modest project provides one of the most refined interpretations of this new typology to date. The common courtyard extends individual workplaces out of doors, and mixed with car parking establishes a no-nonsense sensibility to the plan. The robust character evident in the site planning extends to the exposed steel seismic bracing that provides a distinctive street presence. The matter-of-fact exposed concrete block and repetitive glazing, meanwhile, ensures the persistence of a rational industrial expression that initially formed the neighborhood. Incidentally, the result makes for an excellent foil to the painted timber-framed house next door.

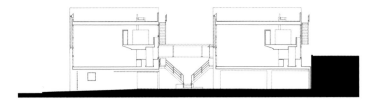

Architect	**Peter Cardew Architects**
Client	**Don Dickson**
Completed	**1998**
Address	**1334 Odlum Drive**
Transit	**VCC Clark + bus 22,**
	Commercial Drive-Broadway + bus 20
Access	**private**

RENFREW PARK

88 RENFREW BRANCH LIBRARY

This urban landscape of largely single-family homes situated on a disciplined gridiron road network, interrupted by schools and modest commercial strips typifies vast areas of greater Vancouver. Among the occasional exceptions to the domestic norm there will typically be some version of a local community centre with associated parkland and recreational facilities. Being Vancouver, the focal point is as likely to be a water park as a skating rink, but even more likely to include an array of activity-focused spaces that have evolved over time. A branch library often forms part of the complex and the multiplicity of uses speaks to the potent continuity of communal values expressed in bricks and mortar as well as in carefully managed social services.

RENFREW BRANCH LIBRARY

On a complex and sloping site, this branch library extends the existing collection of community facilities while offering a more public presence to the overall ensemble at street level. Apart from amplifying the variety of services offered, the new addition facilitates handicapped access, re-orders parking and drop-off arrangements and generally clarifies pedestrian movement in and around the site.

With what may now appear as an almost clichéd West Coast expressive vocabulary – the clarity of articulated structural elements in particular – the project actually was responsible in part for bringing these elements into a common local idiom. Inside, the evocation of a single community space is broken into reading carrels adjacent to perimeter windows, an inner contained media centre, a more intimate children's' area and varied seating configurations among the book storage.

Architect	**Hughes Baldwin Architects**
Structure	**C. Y. Loh Associates Ltd.**
Client	**City of Vancouver, Vancouver Public Library**
Completed	**1994**
Address	**2969 East 22nd Avenue**
Transit	**Nanaimo + bus 25, 29th Ave + bus 16, Renfrew + bus 16**
Access	**public**

OAKRIDGE / SUNSET

Characterized by larger house lots and post-war scaled commercial building, Oakridge's identity is distinctly broad-shouldered in comparison with much of Vancouver. Even the various institutional uses that interrupt the residential gridiron are expansive in nature. Further south, the pattern of commercial high-street resumes along Main Street, which most recently has become the focus for a substantial population with roots in South Asia. There, the ubiquity of the finely grained shop frontages accommodates the interests of varied immigrant groups over time, retaining a degree of familiarity even as the population changes once again.

CELEBRATION HALL

This facility includes administrative offices and consulting rooms, culminating in a communal meeting space with adjacent courtyard. A thoughtful delineation of public and private aspects of the building's program is articulated throughout the complex, with multiple scenarios of use. The entire complex is executed with great care and attention to detail, bringing experiential focus to a considered site strategy on a complex site.

Located within Vancouver's primary municipal cemetery, the construction of the building and attendant landscapes accompanied the provision of extensive new columbaria, giving the entire complex another future generation of service to the community. Extensive use of exposed reinforced concrete with *andesite* stone cladding and paving provide a suitably muted palette that is particularly effective on those occasions when the sky is overcast. The Celebration Hall, while primarily intended as a space for memorials, is also available to the public for diverse gatherings, bringing the activities of the complex into contact with the life of its surrounding community.

Architect	**Birmingham & Wood Architects and Planners**
Landscape	**Phillips Farevaag Smallenberg**
Client	**City of Vancouver**
Completed	**2009**
Address	**5455 Fraser Street**
Transit	**Oakridge-41st Ave + bus 41, or bus 8**
Access	**exterior, limited interior access**

LANGARA COLLEGE LIBRARY & CLASSROOM BUILDING

This new Langara College Library together with smaller installations elsewhere on the Langara campus sets out to differentiate itself from the existing surroundings and present a new visual image for the institution. As a point of focus within the hodge-podge of earlier structures the building is no doubt successful. More generally, the careful consideration of adjacent landscaping conditions suggests promise in describing an articulate ground plane that promotes campus orientation and provides local moments of both pause and informal social interaction.

The project's interior spaces rely largely upon idiosyncratic formal maneuvers to effect interest, with the material surfaces and details rendered very directly. Less obvious to the occupants, the building includes wind towers whose operable fenestration is controlled by a rooftop weather station, contributing to the natural ventilation throughout the interior.

Architect	**Teeple Architects Inc., IBI/HB Architects**
Structure	**Glotman Simpson Consulting Engineers**
Landscape	**Phillips Farevaag Smallenberg**
Client	**Langara College**
Completed	**2007**
Address	**100 West 49th Avenue**
Transit	**Langara-49th Ave**
Access	**college hours**

SUNSET COMMUNITY CENTRE

An array of community services including pre-school, gymnasium and exercise rooms occupy a surprisingly flamboyant structure in the midst of South Main Street's precinct. The diagrammatic simplicity of the plan is rendered with the economies of tilt-wall construction, and given dramatic expression in the curvilinear roofline. Its striking and singular form proudly declares the importance of the building in its surroundings, although offering surprisingly little to the interior suite of rather conventional gathering and support spaces. The building is located adjacent to the Vancouver Park Board's local nursery, and takes a role in alliance with various community educational activities.

Architect	**Bing Thom Architects**
Structure	**Fast + Epp Structural Engineers**
Landscape	**Phillips Farevaag Smallenberg**
Client	**City of Vancouver, Board of Parks & Recreation**
Completed	**2007**
Address	**6810 Main Street**
Transit	**Langara-49th Ave + bus 49, or bus 3**
Access	**public**

Vanier
Park

Sunset
Beach
Park

Pacific

Whyte

Beach

Hornby

Howe

Burrard

Creekside

Pennyfarthing

Duranleau

**Emily Carr
College of
Art & Design**

W 1st

Old Bridge

Johnston

W 2nd

**Waterfall
Building**

Cartwright

W 3rd

W 4th

Sutcliffe
Park

W 5th

Lamey's Mill

W 4th

W 6th

W 6th

W 7th

W 8th

Pine

Fir

Granville

Hemlock

Birch

Alder

W Broadway

0   100 metres

1 minute to walk

W 10th

GRANVILLE ISLAND

Granville Island is an anomaly within the Vancouver urban condition, yet has become fundamental to the array of civic events that characterize the city's identity. Owned by the Canada Mortgage and Housing Corporation and so able to operate outside of market rental forces, the tenants of the island are almost entirely individual business owners. Uses include light industrial and craft production alongside various more deliberately touristic uses, the city's public food market and the central campus of a significant art school.

Due to the singular nature of its ownership and operation, Granville Island exercises a degree of planning constraint extreme even when compared to the rest of Vancouver. As it happens, there has been a very modest degree of new building in the midst of the re-used industrial buildings that characterize the precinct, with the initially rather provisional structures enduring to provide a relatively consistent aesthetic cloak for the now varied public events and uses. The Island serves as a kind of focus for the first era of residential redevelopment of the False Creek industrial lands nearby, and includes its own community centre, for instance. Moreover, its relatively isolated geographic presence ensures that it remains part of a more general civic ownership, happily shared with a myriad of visitors.

EMILY CARR COLLEGE OF ART AND DESIGN

This project sets a high standard in providing sympathetic architectural response to the Island's unique physical context while declaring an undeniably contemporary expression. The public stairway leading to common upper lobby space is executed in appropriately robust fashion, and concludes with a terrific terrace and northern prospect to the downtown skyline. Here the structures of an adjacent concrete batch plant – one of the few industrial uses remaining on the Island – foregrounds a unique view of the city beyond.

The building is also deft in managing its presence adjacent to smaller, unremarkable structures and straddling a multi-level car parking structure. While the fairly blunt reality of corrugated metal panels as a finishing material is sometimes apparent, the overall sense of the building is confident and relaxed. Overall, the project underwrites an ambitious scale of programmatic necessity while maintaining the imperative of accommodating the pedestrian scale so characteristic of Granville Island and the aesthetic imperatives of the enclave's managers.

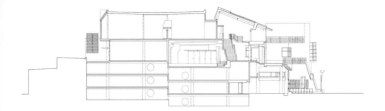

Architect **Patkau Architects**
Client **Emily Carr College of Art and Design, Granville Island Authority**
Completed **1994**
Address **1400 Johnston Street**
Transit **bus 4 or 7 or 50**
Access **college hours**

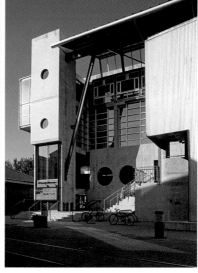

WATERFALL BUILDING

Conceived as a kind of utopian update of Le Corbusier's *Unite d'Habitation*, the project exists as a unique and provocative exception to the conventions of condominium design that dominate Vancouver practice. In its acoustic contribution to the sheltered interior courtyard, the 'waterfall' feature transcends its role as a marketing calling card and actively contributes to the special qualities of the shared hardscape. The attention to urban plan and massing is sufficiently worked through to provide visual depth even on overcast occasions and is executed with a refined palette of carefully considered exposed concrete with aluminum framed doors and windows. Circular staircases rendered in perforated metal give rooftop access to the upper level units, yielding an expressive counterpoint to the otherwise resolute elevations. Not incidentally, they also allow remarkable vistas across False Creek to the city centre.

Architect	**Nick Milkovich Architects Inc. with Arthur Erickson**
Structure	**Fast + Epp Structural Engineers**
Landscape	**Cornelia Hahn Oberlander**
Client	**Hillside Developments**
Completed	**2001**
Address	**1540 West 2nd Avenue**
Transit	**Granville + bus 4, Olympic Village + bus 84**
Access	**public ground level, commercial spaces**

Watermark

2498
Point Grey Rd

Kitsilano
Beach Park

Cornwall

2386 Cornwall

York

Point Grey

W 1st

Tatlow
Park

W 4th

Blenheim

Trutch

Balaclava

Bayswater

MacDonald

Stephens

Trafalgar

Larch

Balsam

Vine

Yew

Arbutus

Maple

Cypress

W Broadway

W 10th

Arbutus Walk

Connaught
Park

W 12th

W 16th

Puget

Carnarvon
Park

Quesnel

Valley

W 19th

W 23rd

Alamein

Trafalgar
Park

Oliver

W King Edward

0   200 metres

2 minutes to walk

KITSILANO

Blessed among Vancouver neighbourhoods with a surfeit of parkland and beach frontage, Kitsilano has also been a pioneer in evolving an urban pattern of single family houses into a mixture of building types with significantly higher population densities. The precinct is a leader within the city in cultivating a true variety of planned residential types – including dedicated projects for seniors – although it still continues to resist the need to distribute low-income and special needs housing outside of the city core.

WATERMARK: KITS BEACH RESTAURANT AND LIFEGUARD FACILITIES

The Watermark represents a first attempt by the Vancouver Park Board to renew and expand upon its waterfront properties through the agency of public-private-partnerships. The ground-level food services together with restrooms and a new lifeguard facility serving adjacent Kitsilano Beach have all been constructed in return for the privileged situation of the private upper-level restaurant. The restaurant also contributes a proportion of its income to help cover maintenance costs for the facility.

Architecturally, the project is thoughtful in execution and conscious of its important role in establishing a new public waterfront setting. The climatic paradoxes that often accompany Vancouver sites provide a particular challenge in the creation of continuous indoor-outdoor spaces with the primary western prospects, encountering glaring afternoon sun and at-times bracing on-shore breezes. Born out of a prolonged and often fractious public consultation, the facility ultimately makes a strong contribution to the daily experience of this significant waterfront site and continues a longstanding tradition of modern formal expression comfortably serving a progressive public agenda.

Architect **AA Robins Architect**
Structure **C.Y. Loh & Associates Ltd**
Landscape **Durante Kreuk Ltd.**
Client **Barnett Company Holdings Ltd., City of Vancouver, Board of Parks and Recreation**
Completed **2005**
Address **1305 Arbutus Street**
Transit **bus 2 or 22**
Access **public**

RESIDENTIAL INFILL

Against the interesting and often ambitious architectural projects chronicled within this guide, there is – of course – a vast array of development and construction that is profoundly conventional. Throughout the single-family neighbourhoods right across the city landscape, ersatz Arts-and-Crafts bungalows abound, interspersed with the generic workhorse referred to as the Vancouver Special.

While the challenging land costs largely discourage experiment and innovation, on Vancouver's West Side, there exists evidence of residential clients committed to cultivating contemporary design in the midst of historically conventional settings.

Address	**2498 Point Grey Road**
Architect	**Bing Thom Architects**
Completed	**1988**
Transit	**bus 2 or 22**
Access	**private**

initiated with Arthur Erickson's seminal project – 2615–17 Point Grey Road – condominiums of comparable scale by Bing Thom – 2498 Point Grey Road – and BattersbyHowat – 2386 Cornwall Avenue – present confident, contemporary expression without antagonizing the sense of scale and material detail of earlier neighbours. Both projects offer refined demonstration of the expressive capabilities of poured-in-place concrete – a hallmark of post-war architecture in Vancouver – to effectively contribute to a domestic scale in building and streetscape.

Address	**2386 Cornwall Avenue**
Architect	**BattersbyHowat,**
	Hancock Bruckner, Eng + Wright
Completed	**2007**
Transit	**bus 2 or 22**
Access	**private**

ARBUTUS WALK

While less conspicuous than other redevelopments of now-redundant industrial land, this project encompasses four city blocks and provides a mix of market, cooperative and senior housing together with attendant parkland and street-level retail accommodations. Unlike related precincts in the downtown peninsula, the general building type is a mid-rise 'slab' construction with underground parking. The extent of the site encouraged development by a number of different design teams on a fragmented property. The result is a variegated portrayal of residential virtue while aggressively adding density to a surrounding neighbourhood of single-family homes and duplexes. In addition to the re-use of the brewery site itself, the project has attracted an array of similarly scaled developments on its perimeter, resulting in a substantial shift in local population density and amplifying the overall sense of expressive diversity.

Among the constituent projects, the New Yorker and 3111 West Eleventh Avenue blocks designed by Nigel Baldwin stand out for their confident material resolution, as does the Arbutus Cooperative complex by the IBI Group. While other components of the precinct are perhaps less distinguished architecturally, the virtues of thoughtful masterplanning at this scale remain evident in the overall experience of the ensemble. The central feature of a common greenway promotes pedestrian activity for a wider constituency, leading westward to connect with the existing amenities of Connaught Park and Kitsilano Community Centre.

Architect	**IBI Group, Nigel Baldwin, Roger Hughes, Downs/Archambault, Howard Bingham Hill, Lawrence Doyle, Richard Henry, Graham Crockart**
Landscape	**Moura Quayle, Durante Kreuk Ltd.**
Client	**Molson Companies Ltd., Concert Properties, Intergulf Investment, Bastion Development, Greystone Properties**
Completed	**1997–2001**
Address	**between 10th Ave, 12th Ave, Vine and Arbutus**
Transit	**bus 9 or 16 or 17**
Access	**public, private residential**

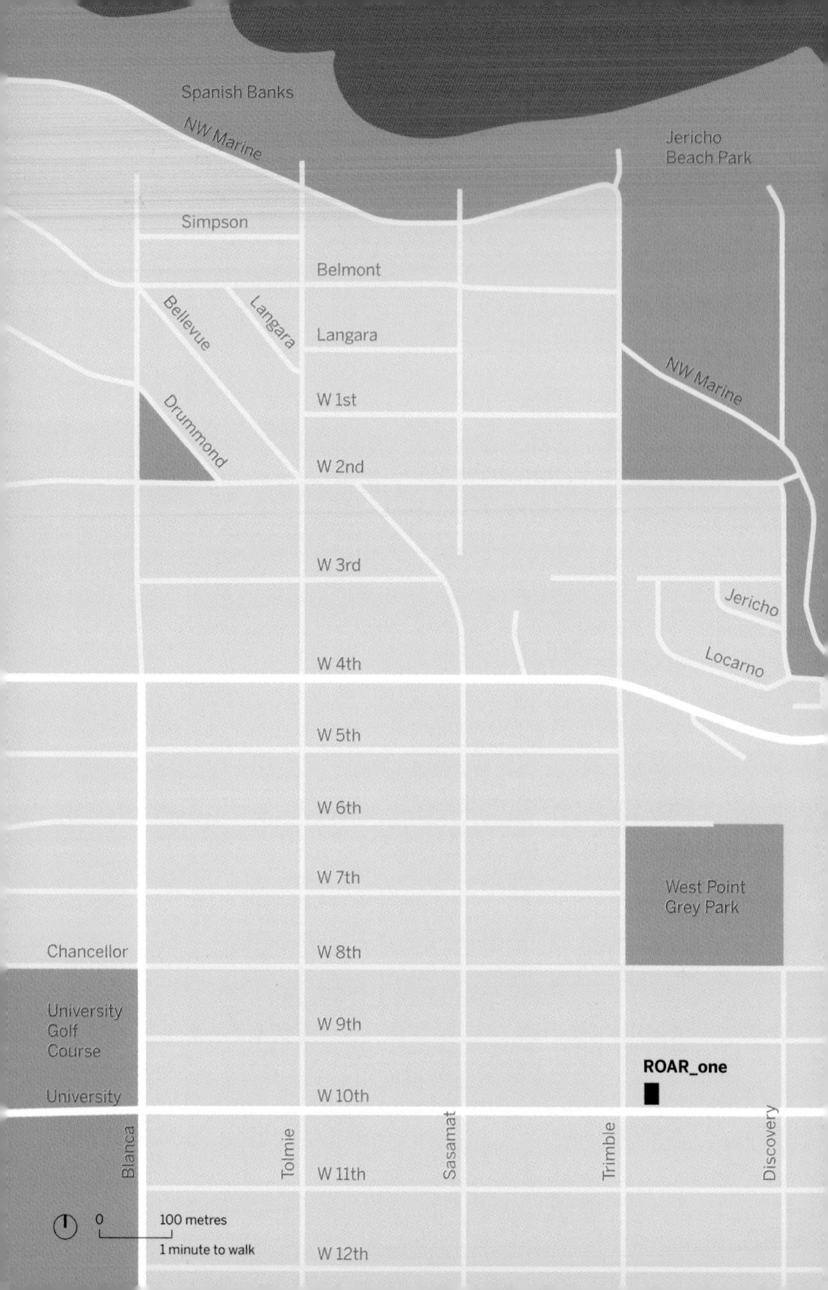

Spanish Banks

NW Marine

Jericho
Beach Park

Simpson

Belmont

Bellevue

Langara

Langara

Drummond

W 1st

W 2nd

NW Marine

W 3rd

Jericho

Locarno

W 4th

W 5th

W 6th

W 7th

West Point
Grey Park

Chancellor

W 8th

University
Golf
Course

W 9th

University

W 10th

ROAR_one
■

Blanca

Tolmie

Sasamat

Trimble

Discovery

W 11th

0   100 metres

1 minute to walk

W 12th

POINT GREY

114 ROAR_one

Vancouver's West Side commercial thoroughfares follow the paths of
pre-war streetcar lines, and were initially home to narrow, single-storey
shops and other commercial services. Contemporary redevelopment has
characteristically presented a pattern of repetitively ordered three-storey
wood framed condominium units above a street-level commercial realm of
concrete construction with levels of car parking below. While in creating a
continuous street wall, the planner's intention was to give the commercial
street its own positive presence, the attendant virtue in providing enclosed
balcony spaces overlooking increasingly busy streets is less compelling.
Architecturally the enactment of this urban planning instinct has tended
towards the conservative and historically referenced.

ROAR_one

This residential project aims to critique the conventional development pattern of multi-family residential constructions – and their attendant assumptions about interior layout – by inviting a more contemporary sense of identity blurred between the domestic and mercantile in double height live-work unit configurations. More significantly, it re-imagines the virtues of external balcony space in the form of tall and deep incursions into the composition of the conventional street frontage. Sliding aluminum screens alternate between privileging the surface continuity of the elevation and public exposure of the patio spaces. In so doing they provide a degree of change and animation unprecedented among adjacent neighbours while contributing to a market housing prototype that has proven to be financially resilient.

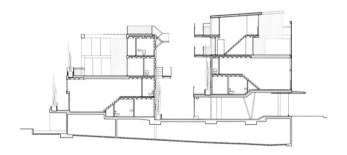

Architect	**LWPAC Lang Wilson Practice in Architecture Culture, Hotson Bakker Boniface Haden Architects**
Client	**ROAR_Ventures Ltd.**
Completed	**2005**
Address	**4387 West 10th Avenue**
Transit	**bus 9 or 17 or 99**
Access	**pubic ground floor commercial spaces**

POINT GREY

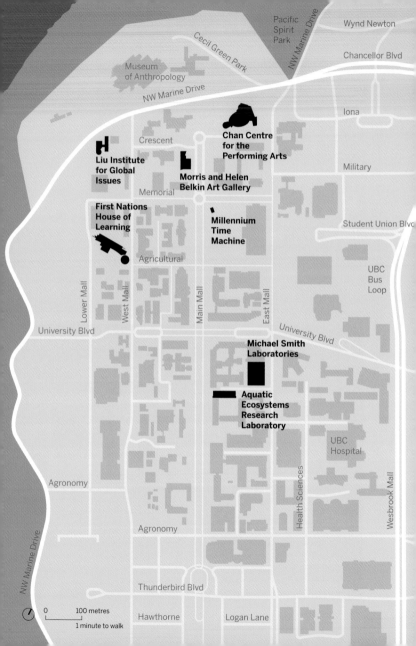

Pacific Spirit Park

Wynd Newton

Cecil Green Park

NW Marine Drive

Chancellor Blvd

Museum of Anthropology

NW Marine Drive

Iona

Crescent

Chan Centre for the Performing Arts

Liu Institute for Global Issues

Morris and Helen Belkin Art Gallery

Military

Memorial

First Nations House of Learning

Millennium Time Machine

Student Union Blvd

Agricultural

UBC Bus Loop

Lower Mall

West Mall

Main Mall

East Mall

University Blvd

University Blvd

Michael Smith Laboratories

Aquatic Ecosystems Research Laboratory

UBC Hospital

Agronomy

Health Sciences

Wesbrook Mall

Agronomy

NW Marine Drive

Thunderbird Blvd

0   100 metres
1 minute to walk

Hawthorne

Logan Lane

UNIVERSITY OF BRITISH COLUMBIA

The University of British Columbia is both blessed and burdened by its extraordinary geographic setting. Set at the end of a peninsula enjoying remarkable views over Howe Sound, the campus at the same time suffers from a high degree of isolation from the city at large. Separated from the nearest neighbourhood by a public park, the UBC campus is obliged perhaps more than any other Canadian university to deliberately establish its own sense of identity.

Efforts to include private sector housing and related services within the University confines have yet to conclude in architecturally significant works, leaving the continuing expansion of academic facilities to declare the University's design ambitions. The desire to exact a measure of public engagement – both with the University community and beyond – is evident in the most accomplished of the recent building projects, and bodes well for future initiatives. The quality of the adjacent housing projects appears dismal and isolated in comparison.

MICHAEL SMITH LABORATORIES

Named in honour of Nobel Prize winning researcher Michael Smith, the building houses research facilities for genomic science and genetic and molecular biology. This functional program is quite literally represented in a mural of colored glazing that is drawn across the length of the primary public façade, representing twelve sequences of a DNA helix. This piece of story-telling is further framed by an external shade structure that shifts the scale of the building beyond the simple repetition of floor levels. This tactic visually enlarges the building's east elevation facing a primary point of campus arrival and clarifies the building's overlap of adjacent structures.

Unusual among UBC campus buildings, a generously proportioned colon-nade further articulates the elevation along East Mall. This public space is deep enough to contain bicycle storage, shelter exterior circulation and accommodate a variety of informal collegial interactions. Inside, a whimsi-cally shaped atrium space – unfortunately not normally accessible to the public – collects the interior life of the building, offering confirmation of the generous spirit that underpins the common arcaded exterior.

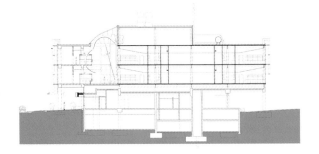

Architect	**Henriquez Partners Architects**
Client	**University of British Columbia**
Completed	**2004**
Address	**2185 East Mall**
Transit	**bus 4 or 9 on W. 4th Avenue,**
	bus 9 or 17 or 99 on W. Broadway
Access	**university hours**

AQUATIC ECOSYSTEMS RESEARCH LABORATORY

This modest classroom and laboratory building sets an agenda for overall planning, drawing the primary entrance back from the Main Mall and creating a continuous covered arcade perpendicular to the Mall. Inside, effort has been made to publicly depict an inner, often hidden, academic life. Within the building's three-storey atrium, suspended skeletons of whales and porpoises provide expressive animation to an entirely restrained material palette. The atrium space offers generous reflected daylight while promoting natural ventilation – an aspect of the environmental poise of the building that is both congruent with and supportive of the building's daily use. Throughout, the building's organization encourages unstructured, local interactions of its inhabitants.

Adjacent, the subsequent construction of the Beaty Biodiversity Research Centre reflects the urban design ambitions of the Ecosystems Laboratory while extending its material and expressive language. Together, the buildings and their contained exterior landscape present a potent model for the campus in which local incident enlivens the daily campus experience and brings the content of academic life into public view.

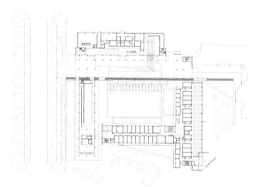

Architect **Patkau Architects**
Landscape **Perry & Associates Inc.**
Client **University of British Columbia**
Completed **2005**
Address **2202 Main Mall**
Transit **bus 4 or 9 on W. 4th Avenue,**
bus 9 or 17 or 99 on W. Broadway
Access **university hours**

FIRST NATIONS HOUSE OF LEARNING

Containing a variety of administrative and meeting rooms, the First Nations House of Learning provides a point of focus for academic and social activities by aboriginal groups on the UBC campus. The structure presents a calculated sense of 'otherness' in its attitudes towards siting, forsaking the alignment to the campus plan for a logic bound to solar orientation, meanwhile respecting the presence of historic arboretum plantings on the site.

In its distinctive expressive vocabulary, the project is rich in its allusion to traditional building traditions and results in a structure that combines the undeniably singular with the very familiar. Most impressively, the material resolution of the building insists upon an experience outside of the usual conventions of institutional buildings. Occupants are invited to consider the regard between the artifice of building and the logics of natural, indigenous forms. This unusual experience is especially poignant in the context of a historically orthodox institution such as UBC.

Architect	**McFarland Marceau Architects**
Landscape	**Phillips Farevaag Smallenberg**
Client	**University of British Columbia**
Completed	**1993**
Address	**1985 West Mall**
Transit	**bus 4 or 9 on W. 4th Avenue,**
	bus 9 or 17 or 99 on W. Broadway
Access	**university hours**

LIU INSTITUTE FOR GLOBAL ISSUES

This substantial extension to the adjacent International House provides direct evidence of two eras of modernist design within UBC's campus experience. The irregular configuration of the primary ground floor meeting area appears first as some kind of geometric residue, yet in its informality proves an effective venue for activities by varied UBC academic groups and – not incidentally – secures the future of existing mature trees on the site. The circular drum of the adjacent formal gathering space is signaled as the Institute's most expressive building element. Inside, the surprising intensity of the space and its ingenious roof structure is thoughtfully withdrawn from the informal adjacent uses.

In the confidence of its material expression the addition draws attention to the considerable changes in technological ability across the two generations of building. Beyond formal and visual comparisons with International House, the Liu Institute embodies virtues of contemporary sustainable building practices, rendered in restrained and confident fashion.

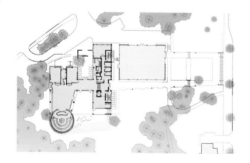

Architect	**Stantec Architecture Ltd. in collaboration with Arthur Erickson**
Landscape	**Cornelia Hahn Oberlander**
Client	**University of British Columbia**
Completed	**2000**
Address	**6476 NW Marine Drive**
Transit	**bus 4 or 9 on W. 4th Avenue, bus 9 or 17 or 99 on W. Broadway**
Access	**university hours**

CHAN CENTRE FOR THE PERFORMING ARTS

While presenting a rather opaque note of arrival to this corner of the campus, the Chan Centre's interior experience is distinctly refined. Including modest 160 and 250 seat 'blackbox' theatres, the 1,400 seat Chan Shun Concert Hall is the undeniable focus of the ensemble. The hall hosts the University's annual convocation ceremonies as well as a variety of public performances throughout the year. Allied with various other educational functions, the building provides one aspect of a concerted effort to invite a broader community to the University setting.

The glazed lobby space collects the varied facilities and in its extension into an adjacent evergreen clearing provides an almost primal counterpoint to the tautly executed geometry of the hall. The interior material palette of exposed concrete, wood panels and plaster surfaces are accented by brass fittings and stainless steel cables that assist in allowing the central overhead roof canopy to accommodate varied acoustic requirements.

Architect	**Bing Thom Architects**
Acoustics	**ARTEC**
Theatre	**Theatre Projects Inc.**
Landscape	**Cornelia Hahn Oberlander, Elizabeth Watts**
Client	**University of British Columbia**
Completed	**1997**
Address	**6265 Crescent Road**
Transit	**bus 4 or 9 on W. 4th Avenue,**
	bus 9 or 17 or 99 on W. Broadway
Access	**exterior, interior lobby**

MORRIS AND HELEN BELKIN ART GALLERY

Along with the Museum of Anthropology, the Morris and Helen Belkin Art Gallery serves as a primary public exhibition venue for the University. While taking material cues for its exterior white brickwork from earlier structures nearby, the Gallery is vigorous in modeling its various interior roles and declaring their relationships in its external form. Within, substantial partition walls are able to rotate in order to provide flexible configurations of the primary exhibition space.

Set at one extreme of the campus' Main Mall, this modestly scaled building is challenged to resolve the condition of a free-standing pavilion – each elevation essentially a 'front' – with the necessity of providing substantial back-of-house servicing. The resulting loading bay facing directly across a courtyard space to the lobby of the University's Frederic Wood Theatre concludes with uncertain resolution. In this, the Gallery speaks to the more general difficulty of constructing a coherent public realm from the consequence of providing singular, individual buildings.

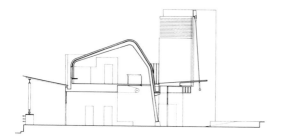

Architect	**Peter Cardew Architects**
Structure	**C.Y. Loh & Associates Ltd.**
Client	**University of British Columbia**
Completed	**1995**
Address	**1825 Main Mall**
Transit	**bus 4 or 9 on W. 4th Avenue,** **bus 9 or 17 or 99 on W. Broadway**
Access	**public**

MILLENIAL TIME MACHINE

Forming one component of the Belkin Art Gallery's outdoor campus art tour, this pavilion in miniature was crafted as a Canada Council for the Arts millennial legacy project, and houses Rodney Graham's mobile *camera obscura* embodied in a carefully restored nineteenth century laundau carriage. The meticulous detail of the building – and indeed of the restored carriage – presents an artifact of considerable refinement, although with the perhaps inadvertent result of presenting a stridently formal presentation of the work.

The skewed orientation of the pavilion results from the camera's focus on a nearby young sequoia tree. Added to the very occasional animation of occupants in the building this eccentricity contributes to the pavilion's enigmatic presence within the experience of the campus' Main Mall.

Architect **superkül architecture**
Structure **Fast + Epp Structural Engineers**
Client **Morris and Helen Belkin Art Gallery**
Completed **2003**
Address **1940 Main Mall**
Transit **bus 4 or 9 on W. 4th Avenue,**
bus 9 or 17 or 99 on W. Broadway
Access **public, interior access by appointment**

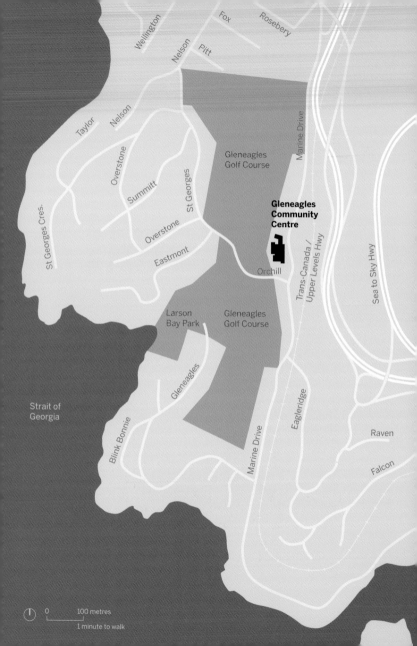

GLENEAGLES

134 GLENEAGLES COMMUNITY CENTRE

Overlooking the Strait of Georgia, this is an area in which many of the more daring and formative early modern houses of Vancouver were constructed – in part because the challenging terrain discouraged traditional builders while inspiring local architects to be inventive. The combination of verdant landscape and extreme topography results in meandering streets with occasional glimpses of harbour below. It continues to invite spirited contemporary design responses.

GLENEAGLES COMMUNITY CENTRE

The Gleneagles Community Centre accommodates a full array of community functions, including central gymnasium, fitness, childcare and administrative facilities. Located on a sloping site, the building acts as a kind of resilient buttress and provides direct access to local outdoor spaces for virtually all major program elements. The resulting juxtaposition between logics of site and the demands of internal functions results in a series of eccentrically disposed spaces, visually linked across internal glazed partitions. Whether in the sectional bias of the basketball court or the experience of exercise bikes within the building's 'eaves', the strategic response to context results in an assertive challenge to assumptions about organizing recreational spaces. An innovative integration of structure and services recognizes environmental imperatives from the outset and – significantly – will reduce longer term operating costs.

The building's position on a major local thoroughfare amplifies its public identity, although the suburban reality of arrival by car undermines any intended sense of clear sequential entry. The characteristically thoughtful material detail no doubt contributes to the pleasure of the Centre's occupants, and as elsewhere in greater Vancouver renders the positive virtues of community building in a significant, articulate architectural statement.

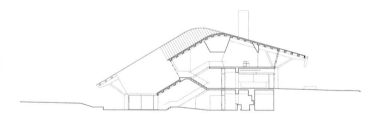

Architect	**Patkau Architects**
Consultants	**Fast + Epp Structural Engineers**
Client	**District of West Vancouver**
Completed	**2003**
Address	**6262 Marine Drive**
Transit	**bus 250 – lengthy trip by public transit**
Access	**public**

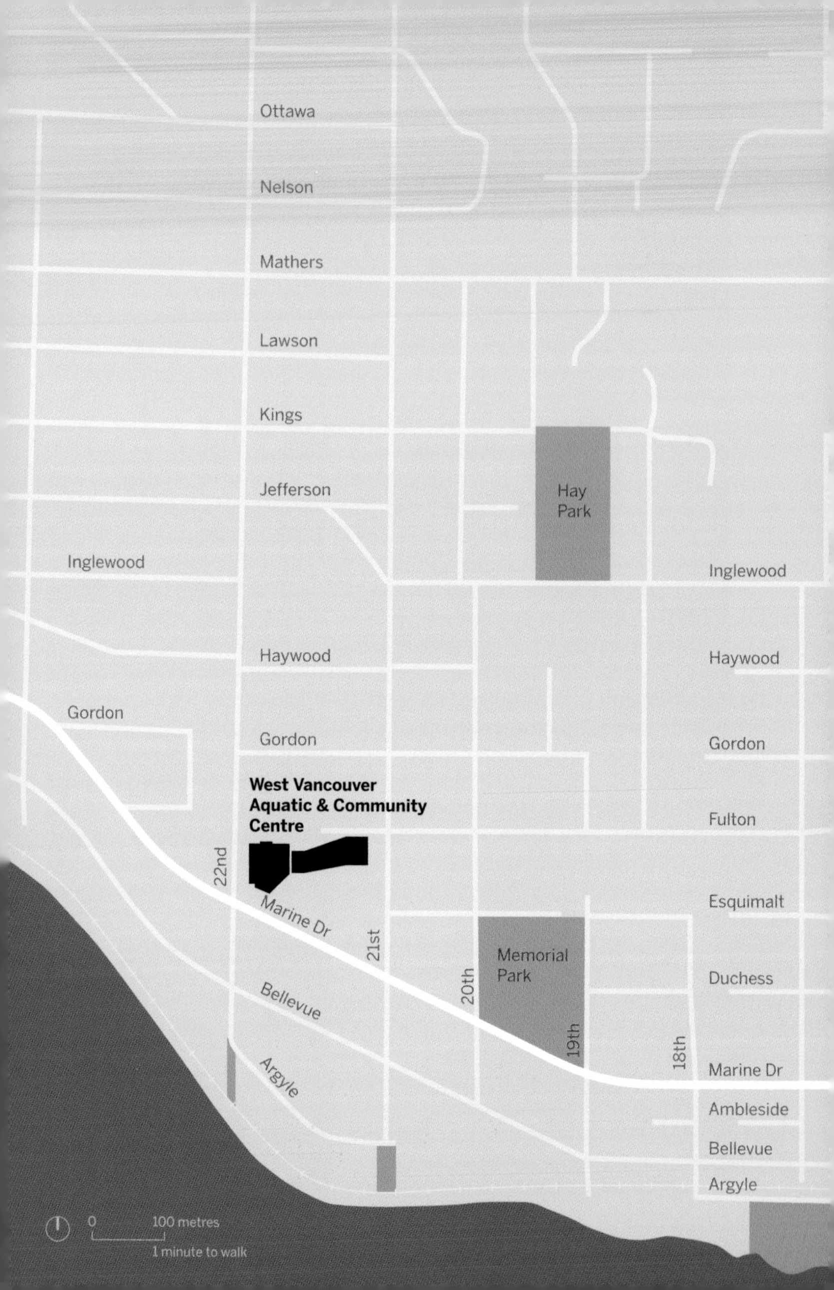

Ottawa

Nelson

Mathers

Lawson

Kings

Jefferson

Hay
Park

Inglewood

Inglewood

Haywood

Haywood

Gordon

Gordon

Gordon

Gordon

**West Vancouver
Aquatic & Community
Centre**

Fulton

22nd

Marine Dr

21st

20th

Esquimalt

Memorial
Park

Duchess

Bellevue

19th

18th

Argyle

Marine Dr

Ambleside

Bellevue

Argyle

0   100 metres

1 minute to walk

DUNDARAVE

138 WEST VANCOUVER AQUATIC & COMMUNITY CENTRE

Located just beyond West Vancouver's central commercial precinct of Ambleside – the original site for ferry crossings from Vancouver – the Dundarave area presently serves as one part of the urban focus for the immediate region. Most notably, the denser residential towers that stretch westward from Lion's Gate Bridge are here held at bay, contributing to an effective pedestrian scale even alongside the major traffic artery of Marine Drive. While resolutely local in emphasis and suburban in tone, the area is evolving to discover its own distinct character and complexity.

WEST VANCOUVER AQUATIC & COMMUNITY CENTRE

This two-phased project containing aquatic centre, related recreational facilities and attendant service elements provides confident expression for the community of West Vancouver. Most directly, a dramatic expanse of glass faces onto the main commercial street of the area, affording tantalizing views of the interior to passing motorists while at the same time offering distant and dramatic views across Vancouver's harbour to swimmers on top of the waterslide. The extensive provision of natural lighting allied with operable glazed overhead doors and vents enables natural ventilation and contributes to an overall exterior character through-out the primary public areas. Both inside and out the careful attention to material detail helps to ameliorate the inevitably coarse scale of the broad-shouldered recreational spaces. This concern for detail is also manifest in the project's sophisticated mechanical systems and insistence upon providing universal accessibility to the pools themselves.

The provision of new recreational facilities also aims to establish a more distinctly urban presence for the local community. In contrast to the symbolic presence addressing Marine Drive, on the interior a public plaza is formed overtop of the Centre's parking garage. Even when vacant, this space suggests a potential for civic gathering, and in so doing grants the daily occasion of entrance a more special and communal experience.

Architect	**Hughes Condon Marler Architects**
Structure	**Fast + Epp Structural Engineers**
Landscape	**Phillips Farevaag Smallenberg**
Client	**District of West Vancouver**
Completed	**2004**
Address	**2121 Marine Drive**
Transit	**bus 250**
Access	**public, www.westvancouver.net**

BRITISH PROPERTIES

If extravagant topography seems commonplace throughout Vancouver, the juxtaposition of mountainside and waterfront is nowhere as intense as it is in West Vancouver. This results in a certain kind of urban ecology in which the transportation logic of Marine Drive, the Upper Level Highway and Lion's Gate Bridge stakes out the primary order of the city. The grain of the city expands as the elevation rises, until public parkland and golf courses merge with truly natural mountain landscapes.

HAR-EL SYNAGOGUE

This project carefully orchestrates a program that includes worship space, library and classrooms as well as areas specifically devoted to both youths and seniors. Composed and exercised with confident material resolve, the Synagogue enjoys the special virtue of being a discreet destination within its surrounding suburban landscape. Located at the intersection of two busy highways and a salmon spawning creek, the sequence of approach from highway to parking lot to front entry is rehearsed with a dramatic alliance between the architecture and its compelling surroundings. The canopy awaiting arrival across stream and bridge speaks directly to the building's desire to accommodate while meanwhile cultivating a sense of ritual.

The subsequent interior experience of community event spaces is tersely detailed and robust. The desire for exterior clarity is privileged to the extent that specific interior relationships are effectively camouflaged from outside view, yet the abiding experience of the project is positive, dignified and convivial.

Architect	**Acton Ostry Architects**
Structure	**Glotman Simpson Consulting Engineers**
Client	**Congregation Har-El**
Completed	**1998**
Address	**1305 Taylor Way**
Transit	**bus 254**
Access	**public, some restrictions**

THE WOODS COLUMBARIA

This modest project accommodates niches and family columbaria within the setting of a larger municipal cemetery. Approached across a public park and set within a stand of conifers, a series of courtyards and covered resting places intercede in the woodland experience, with the remains of a fallen tree serving as the empty centre of the ensemble. Small – apparently incidental – water pools catch rainwater and reflect the points of sky through the trees overhead, adding to the overall setting of mourning and contemplation. In deferring to the existing conditions of the landscape, an informality of organization is maintained through which the designed artifacts appear increasingly grounded in their place as time passes.

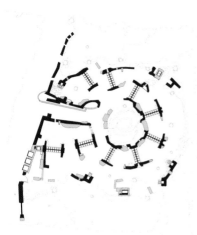

Architect **Pechet and Robb Art and Architecture Ltd.**
Client **Capilano View Cemetery, District of West Vancouver**
Completed **1993**
Address **1490 3rd Street**
Transit **not easily accessible by public transit**
Access **public**

LONSDALE

Once a thriving industrial port, the waterfront heart of North Vancouver has been undergoing a transformation every bit as radical as Vancouver's Coal Harbour or False Creek, albeit in a less frantically paced mode. The juxtapositions of scales of building can be dramatic as large parcels of industrial land spawn major development projects virtually adjacent to traditional single-family streets. The combination of easy ferry access to downtown Vancouver with geographic proximity to the recreational amenities of the North Shore Mountains give the area a very distinct sense of place even as it attains a more urban density and character.

THE PIER

On the northern shore of Burrard Inlet, adjacent to the seabus ferry terminal, this important public space serves as the common landscape to a massive redevelopment of the Burrard Shipyards. While literally acres of amenity space have been created during the course of recent development, the degree of accompanying design attention has largely proven to be disappointing. Providing exception to the rule, this elaboration of a waterside precinct provides an engaging combination of ground-level surface treatment with deftly realized designs for urban furnishings, lighting and staging for public events.

References to the materials of the industrial past are lighthearted and encourage the informal and often unpredictable occasions that might occupy such a terrain. The overall result is a collective landscape that asserts a potent sense of geographic locale while inviting a variety of social activities to unfold.

Architect	**Pechet and Robb Art and Architecture Ltd., Durante Kreuk Ltd.**
Client	**City of North Vancouver**
Completed	**2005**
Address	**lower Lonsdale along the waterfront**
Transit	**Seabus**
Access	**public**

NORTH VANCOUVER CITY LIBRARY

The new North Vancouver City Library establishes its importance in the local community through its central location and its very conscious effort to use transparency to literally denote accessibility. Apart from extensively expanding the capacity of the previous library, the building provides an assertive expression of North Vancouver's own sense of new-found urbanity. Adjacent to the Library's main entry, a portion of pedestrianised street has been transformed into an informal public plaza, enclosed to the south by the adjacent City Hall. The varied landscape treatment includes wireless café terrace, amphitheatre and outdoor reading rooms, offering a strong sense of occasion to the new building without undermining the scale of adjacent pedestrian realms.

Inside the building is executed with restraint, and provides an entirely appropriate openness and ease of circulation, focused on a sky-lit central atrium. This demonstration of a welcoming ambience culminates in the surprising presence of an exterior roof-level terrace. This public verandah beautifully extends the generosity of the ground level plaza in providing the prospect of harbour and city for all.

Architect	**Diamond + Schmitt Architects Inc., CEI Architecture**
Landscape	**Phillips Farevaag Smallenberg**
Client	**City of North Vancouver**
Completed	**2008**
Address	**120 West 14th Street**
Transit	**bus 230**
Access	**public, www.cnv.org/nvcl**

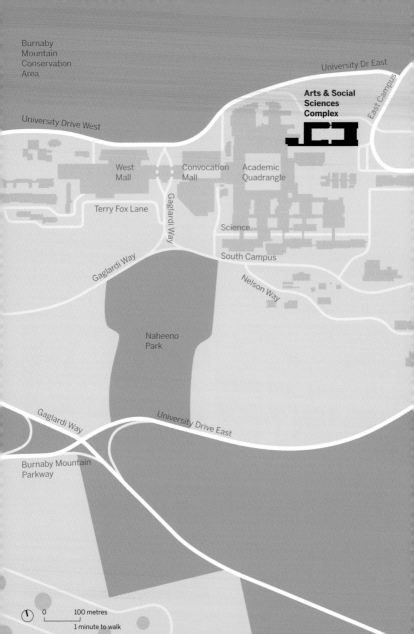

Burnaby
Mountain
Conservation
Area

University Dr East

**Arts & Social
Sciences
Complex**

East Campus

University Drive West

West
Mall

Convocation
Mall

Academic
Quadrangle

Gaglardi Way

Terry Fox Lane

Gaglardi Way

Science

South Campus

Nelson Way

Naheeno
Park

Gaglardi Way

University Drive East

Burnaby Mountain
Parkway

0   100 metres

1 minute to walk

SIMON FRASER UNIVERSITY

154 ARTS & SOCIAL SCIENCES COMPLEX

The inspired master plan for Simon Fraser University was the result of a competition won by Arthur Erickson and his partner Geoffrey Massey in 1963. The university opened with an incoming enrollment of 2000 two years later. Now an institution with over 20,000 students, SFU has sites in Surrey as well as in Vancouver's downtown east side at the new Woodward's site. The home base on Burnaby Mountain remains a central focus.

Most recently augmented by residential development on the perimeter of the academic precinct, the campus continues to be largely ordered and inspired by the Erickson and Massey planning logic. While the plan has been implemented in the form of architectural projects by a whole generation of Vancouver designers, Convocation Mall remains the most compelling testament to that initial vision, as the memorial service to Arthur Erickson in summer 2009 bore eloquent witness.

The overall experience speaks to the campus' historical origins, presenting the most sustained evidence of the marriage between late-modern Brutalism and Canada's West Coast reinforced concrete building culture. Most recently, the expanded residential programme and new academic facilities further demonstrate the potent planning logic of the competition scheme while providing new expressive and material palettes.

ARTS & SOCIAL SCIENCES COMPLEX

This substantial project comprises a virtual University in itself, including facilities for Schools of Archaeology, Criminology, Clinical Psychology, First Nations Studies and the Faculty of Health Sciences – all accommodated in a series of phased constructions. Site planning shows an alliance with contemporary sustainable building practices, but also demonstrates support for the logic of Erickson and Massey's original campus masterplan and the original buildings' rhythmic expression of structure.

This being said, the material vocabulary is very evidently of *our* time and provides relief to the consistent concrete expression that characterizes so much of the campus. Interiors are crisp and largely daylit, with a consistent emphasis upon public circulation areas that double up as informal social spaces. The sustainability agenda is pursued across various scales, including natural ventilation and solar control, green roofing, heat recovery systems and water and energy efficient fixtures throughout. Overall, the complex establishes a new benchmark for design and environmental performance for future academic buildings.

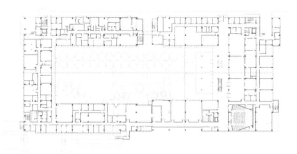

Architect	**Busby Perkins+Will**
Structure	**Fast + Epp Structural Engineers**
Landscape	**Phillips Farevaag Smallenberg**
Client	**Simon Fraser University**
Completed	**2008**
Address	**8888 University Drive**
Transit	**bus 135**
Access	**university hours**

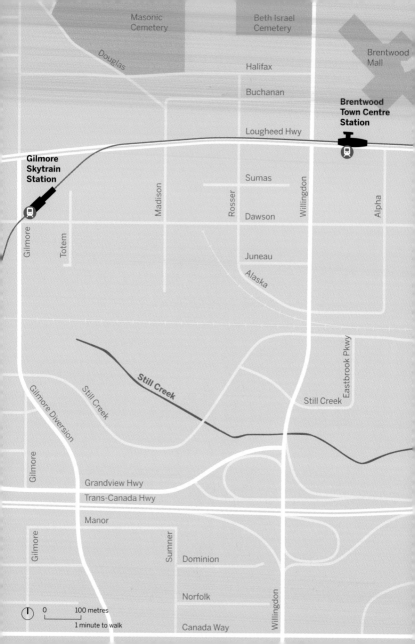

BURNABY

Sandwiched between Vancouver and its neighbouring municipalities, Burnaby has been strongly shaped by the presence of east-west transportation corridors of varied scales, including local commercial streets, larger arterial roads and the Trans Canada Highway. The development impetus of the Skytrain construction has made these roadways even more important and encouraged a new density to fill in a largely diffuse post-war urban landscape – most evident in the aggregation of building known as Metrotown. Against the coarse grain of the existing city structure, a number of distinct urban centres have been planned, and are now being realized with varying degrees of success.

BRENTWOOD TOWN CENTRE STATION

The most sculptural and iconic of the Millenium Line Skytrain stations, the structure at Brentwood responds to the challenge to create a signature station. The canoe-shaped plan provides a direct and efficient map of circulation needs, with connections to ground level and bridging across the Lougheed Highway to connect with an adjacent shopping centre. The station is covered with a double curved roof form constructed of glulam beams and solid 2x4 'shell', with glass panels on each side that provide views of the surrounding landscape. When illuminated at night, in particular, the building provides eloquent expression to what might otherwise be a straightforward resolution of transportation infrastructure.

Architect	**Busby Perkins+Will**
Structure	**Fast + Epp Structural Engineers**
Landscape	**Durante Kreuk Ltd.**
Public Art	**Jill Anholt**
Client	**Rapid Transit Project Office**
Completed	**2002**
Address	**4533 Lougheed Highway**
Access	**public**

GILMORE SKYTRAIN STATION

Balancing the exuberance of the Brentwood Station the nearby Gilmore Station is a model of restraint. This modesty of means presented its own challenge and the architects together with structural engineers Fast + Epp have created a structure of considerable elegance. The station features a roof system consisting of pretensioned curved roof panels supported by a simple structural steel frame. The repetition of smaller scaled elements contributes to an experience very different in scale from the more singular Brentwood station, yet every bit as satisfying in bringing a level of material ambition to the task.

Architect	**Busby Perkins+Will**
Consultants	**Fast + Epp Structural Engineers**
Landscape	**Durante Kreuk Ltd.**
Public Art	**Muse Atelier**
Client	**Rapid Transit Project Office**
Completed	**2001**
Address	**2199 Gilmore Ave**
Access	**public**

SURREY

Surrey, British Columbia's second largest city, has a population growth that outpaces that of Vancouver, although its urban landscape remains largely post-war suburban sprawl. Motivated by its engagement to a larger-scale, regional transportation planning process, local government is actively encouraging greater density through greater diversity of use. As Vancouver has become the paradigm for rethinking traditional down-town precincts, perhaps Surrey can in due course become the model for reconfiguring the urban periphery.

SURREY CENTRAL CITY

Surrey Central City is an ambitious mixed use project that is grafted onto an existing, aging shopping mall. The design provides vivid counterpoint to the original closed, rectilinear format deliberately extending the pedestrian landscape around a five-storey tall atrium space. This galleria volume is capped with an engineered-wood roof structure supporting skylights that allow natural light into the mall below.

The galleria is linked horizontally through a system of bridges to the shapely office tower and presents a new glazed entry façade supported by tapered columns of composite timber. Connecting office tower, galleria and podium are three floors of a satellite branch of Simon Fraser University. In both form and exterior surface treatment – a mélange of metal paneling – the project declares its progressive identity. The project's present context insists on an experience that remains more suburban office park than central city, although poised as a catalyst for a more urbane surrounding development.

Architect	**Bing Thom Architects**
Structure	**Jones Kwong Kishi, Structure Craft Builders Inc.**
Client	**Insurance Corporation of British Columbia (ICBC)**
Completed	**2002**
Address	**13450 102 Avenue**
Transit	**Surrey Central, King George**
Access	**public**

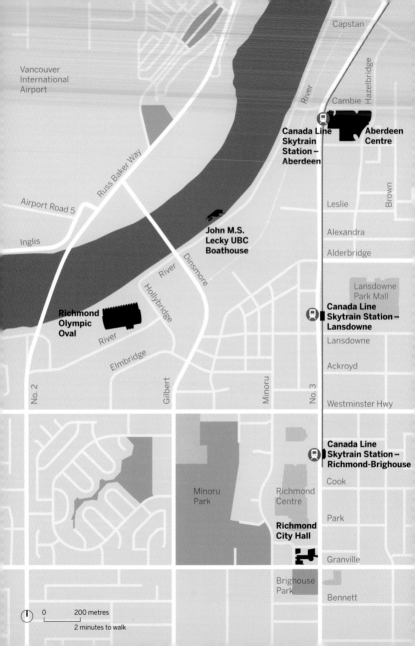

RICHMOND

The City of Richmond's geographic character is almost antithetical to that of Vancouver. Flat, alluvial and agriculturally productive lands are surrounded by earthwork dikes built to prevent floods and the channels of the Fraser River. Traditionally devoted to industrial and transportation uses, the Fraser River remains for most inhabitants of greater Vancouver a hidden and enigmatic landscape. While the redevelopment of industrial and railway lands on Burrard Inlet and False Creek has played a critical role in defining Vancouver's contemporary urban character, the comparable redevelopment of the banks of the Fraser has so far been more piecemeal and essentially private.

Richmond as well serves as the site for Vancouver's International Airport, conspiring with local soil conditions to effect a comparatively modest building height restriction as well as discouraging Vancouver's more general habit of constructing underground parking. The net result is a very different urban landscape, measured by lingering increments of agricultural use and occupied to a significant degree by recent Asian immigrants. Aggravated by the recent arrival of the Canada Line rapid transit connection to downtown Vancouver, the result is a central core poised between *American Graffiti* and *Blade Runner* – potentially the most compelling urban tableau in metropolitan Vancouver's future.

JOHN M.S. LECKY UBC BOATHOUSE

This floating two-storey structure, located in the Middle Arm of the Fraser River, houses storage and docks for the launching of rowing shells, dragon boats and motorized coach boats. Support facilities and a publicly accessible function room populate the upper floor, and the overall composition makes an important contribution to the revitalization of the adjacent dike as a regional amenity. Various communities of boaters enjoy the facility and are quite literally thrust upon the geography of the river.

In particular, the building's participants – upstairs and down – are granted a view upstream that offers a unique perspective on the significance of the Fraser in Vancouver's urban form. The juxtaposition of what are effectively industrial uses at water level with the administrative and public interiors above has been carefully managed in both the form and material manner of the building. Importantly, the sense of being on the water and disentangled from the adjacent shore is present in all aspects of the building's use.

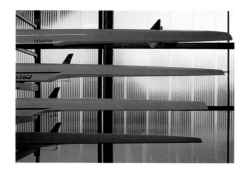

Architect	**McFarland Marceau Architects**
Structure	**Fast + Epp Structural Engineers**
Client	**University of British Columbia**
Completed	**2007**
Address	**7277 River Road**
Transit	**Aberdeen**
Access	**public**

RICHMOND OLYMPIC OVAL

The Olympic Oval is without question the most ambitious of the various structures designed and built in anticipation of the 2010 Winter Olympics, and consolidates an ambitious planning strategy for the City of Richmond. In sponsoring the construction of the facility, the City of Richmond projected its future use as a major community amenity housing varied sporting activities and stimulating future occupation of an industrial landscape as public parkway. Allied with plans for adjacent market housing, the building and its surrounds suggest the compelling potential of a series of public occasions linked along the length of the riverside.

Inside, the vast volume of the primary competition space has been created – in collaboration with structural engineers Fast + Epp – with a truly extraordinary structural and material palette. Spanning nearly 100 metres, the secondary roof structure is assembled from plywood and 2x4 dimensional lumber milled from the vast areas of forest destroyed by the mountain pine beetle. The result is a richly textured visual surface that in the absence of more muscular structural elements appears to very nearly defy gravity.

Architect	**Cannon Design Architecture Inc.**
Structure	**Fast + Epp Structural Engineers, Glotman Simpson**
Roof Design	**Structure Craft Builders Inc.**
Client	**City of Richmond**
Completed	**2008**
Address	**6111 River Road**
Transit	**Richmond-Brighouse + bus 401 or 407 or C94**
Access	**public**

RICHMOND CITY HALL

As Richmond's population grows, the City Hall serves to express a sense of civic pride and anticipates an emerging consolidation of urban density. The extensive range of program elements is represented as four distinct building components: an administrative tower, the council chamber, the meeting house and a connective galleria. Beyond the sum of the parts, the project creates an ensemble of meticulously landscaped public spaces that judiciously balance inviting informality with a sense of public occasion. The water gardens in particular contribute to the sense of calm and reserve, contributing to a concern for sustainability that informs the working conditions of the inhabitants as much as it does the mechanical services.

While evidence of Richmond's growth is conspicuous everywhere, the Centro condominium project south-east of the City Hall across No 3 Road – executed by the same design team – offers a clear and immediate sense of the new urban scale that the civic centre anticipates.

Architect	**Hotson Bakker Boniface Haden Architects, Kuwabara Payne McKenna Blumberg Architects**
Landscape	**Phillips Farevaag Smallenberg**
Client	**City of Richmond**
Completed	**2002**
Address	**6911 No. 3 Road**
Transit	**Richmond-Brighouse**
Access	**exterior, interior lobby**

CANADA LINE SKYTRAIN STATIONS

The third and most recent expansion of Vancouver's largely elevated rapid transit system connects the city's downtown with the airport and the northern sector of the City of Richmond. The station design is generally more restrained than that of the Millenium Line and the three stations along Richmond's No. 3 Road in particular strive to present a familial similarity to one another. With their extensive use of glass and timber roof canopies set against the reinforced concrete of the skytrain track supports, the structures present what is for the Vancouver region a familiar material palette confidently executed.

Perhaps as important as the stations themselves is their role in anticipating – and enabling – subsequent development within their surrounding urban landscapes. The glimpses of a more dense environment that occur else-where in Richmond will almost certainly be echoed in the transformation of suburban shopping malls and single storey warehouses to describe a new chapter of Vancouver urbanism.

Architect	**Busby Perkins+Will**
Structure	**Fast + Epp Structural Engineers**
Client	**InTransitBC**
Completed	**2009**
Address	**No. 3 Road + Cambie, No. 3 Road + Lansdowne, No. 3 Road between Cook & Saba**
Transit	**Aberdeen, Lansdowne, Richmond-Brighouse**
Access	**public, with paid fare**

ABERDEEN CENTRE

This commercial shopping centre deliberately challenges a number of assumptions about the conventional suburban mall, and in doing so successfully creates something of a monument within its surrounding landscape. Most obviously the sinuous, glazed and brightly coloured exterior elevations establish a degree of transparency from street to interior – and vice versa – that is antithetical to the normally opaque presentation of North American malls. This effort to provide light and a sense of open accessibility is further pursued in the interior, with an extraordinary degree of overhead natural light complementing the illumination from the perimeter. Organizationally, the mall consists only of smaller individual merchants supporting the ambition of creating a texture of experience quite different from the traditional logic of primary retail anchors.

Although the conventions of material palette and construction systems differ little from conventional shopping mall typologies, the structure is unquestionably successful in achieving a distinct and memorable identity in a context that remains conspicuously uneventful. In particular, the decision to take the edge of the project to the adjacent sidewalk results in this usually distant building type – habitually absent from urban life – firmly engaged with the emerging experience of the new city of Richmond.

Architect	**Bing Thom Architects**
Client	**Fairchild Development**
Completed	**2004**
Address	**4151 Hazelbridge Way**
Transit	**Aberdeen**
Access	**public**

SUPERMODEL
MATTHEW SOULES

It's 8:00 am, the elevator door opens, and there he is – just beyond the lobby's glass. Only yesterday I caught a glimpse of him when he was gliding between the towers, his reflection ricocheting across the countless window walls. Now he seems consumed with foraging the sub-surface depths of our building's roof-top pond. Strange when you think about it, at this moment many of my thousands of neighbors in this forest of condominiums are aligned with this bird, this Great Blue Heron – connected by a common activity occurring in shared proximity; eating breakfast. By the time I get down to the sea-wall, the joggers are out in force. And the ocean, wow, it's so calm – totally serene. Kayakers already! Doesn't anybody work? I've read that this part of city is the second densest in North America. How can that be? It feels so spacious … so orderly. And the mountains, I can see them so easily. By the time I finish the short walk to my office it's practically impossible to suppress the feeling that this place, this city, just might be utopia.

Utopia!? How is this feeling possible? We all know that utopia can't *exist*. But the sentiment persists and proliferates. In recent years city-makers from Dubai to Dallas have come to view Vancouver as an urban paradise and now seek to more or less imitate it. During the time-span covered by this guidebook Vancouver has emerged as an unlikely archetype, a place that cities everywhere look to as *the* prime example of the 'Livable City.' Vancouver is a *supermodel*.

Much of the city's utopian character derives from its spectacular location. Where else does such a relatively large and dynamic metropolitan condition exist in immediate proximity to beaches, rainforests, and snow-capped peaks? Where else can we witness high-density urbanism co-existing with such vibrant and healthy natural ecologies? Deer filled forests sit right at the city's edge. Waters within the metropolis teem with millions of migrating salmon. But it's not the city's fortuitous siting alone that has garnered so much attention. Architecture, urban design, and planning have capitalized on the city's natural assets to produce an exceptional built environment that has secured its supermodel status.

Part of Vancouver's anomaly arises from the fact that it is dizzyingly new. If you're going to build utopia you need the opportunity. Within the period of this guidebook the city's population has ballooned by more than 67%. Since 1995 more than 150 high-rise residential towers have been built in the downtown peninsula in what constitutes a radical and whole-sale transformation of central Vancouver. A bulk of these towers are located in two master-planned communities, Concord Pacific Place on the north shore of False Creek and Coal Harbour to the west of the Central Business District, and together they cover an astounding one-sixth of the downtown peninsula. Few cities in recent decades have been so significantly and directly determined by master-planned urban design. These two neighbourhoods, along with areas of the city they have inspired, have come to define Vancouver as the apotheosis of contemporary urban livability. Glassy, slender, and well- spaced podium towers maximize views and light while enlivening the sidewalk. The public seawall and a generous amount of parks and civic amenities offer recreation, leisure, and community-life all within easy walking distance. It is a safe, clean, calm, and highly designed form of urbanism. It also registers the logics and modes of globalization.

At the dawn of the 21st Century there is no such thing as a non-global city. Globalization has impacted everywhere ... even Antarctica. Nevertheless, the degree to which the heightened liquidity in people, goods, and money has informed supermodel Vancouver is remarkable for its legibility. The population explosion that has fuelled Vancouver's make-over has been determined to a large degree by remote geopolitical events and international migration – the city was, for instance, a primary destination for the pre-1997 exodus from Hong Kong. The speed and scale of Vancouver's development entails construction financing made possible through the workings of global capital – Concord Pacific Place, for example, was built with money from Asia. A not insignificant number of condominium units are purchased by foreign investors, and many condominuim towers have been primarily marketed in foreign cities. In these ways, the thicket of towers that represents supermodel Vancouver is the iconic and palpable result of globalization.

More significant, however, is that the very concept of 'livability' for which new Vancouver is famed is itself a manifestation of globalization's dominant worldview. As an ideological condition that is founded upon liberalism and capitalism, globalization prefaces a lifestyle urbanism that is shaped by the preoccupations of the influence-wielding upper middle class. Situated within this ideological context Vancouver's livability translates into an urbanism that elevates fitness, leisure, and comfort as the ultimate barometers of city life. This value system synthesizes perfectly with Vancouver's natural setting. Activities such as jogging on the seawall or sipping a cappuccino while taking in a natural vista emerge as ideal urban behaviour. Architecture and urban design that facilitate this experiential symbiosis between lifestyle and nature not only belong to the condominium mega-developments—the contours of this livability can be traced to buildings throughout the city.

While glass and transparency are a common preoccupation of contemporary architecture almost everywhere, their role is more deeply entrenched in Vancouver. This phenomenon results from the combined impact of the natural landscape and livability on the Vancouver psyche and allows Vancouver architecture to achieve multiple effects. Of course, it facilitates the view. Building types that are usually hermetic become open. The

Olympic Speed Skating Oval with its vast north facing glazing opens up to the North Shore Mountains that rise in the distance. The Vancouver Convention Centre's West Building exposes its circulation and break-out spaces to the harbour. But the provision of views is only the most obvious implication of glass. At a more fundamental and pervasive level the prominent role of glass serves to diminish the schism between the interior and exterior. If the interior is the primary domain of architecture, it belongs to the artificial world, while the exterior, in the broadest sense, belongs to nature. Glazing merges these domains by minimizing their threshold of separation. The relative immateriality of glass also allows architecture to flirt with non-materiality, and ultimately, non-existence. This signals perhaps a latent desire within much of Vancouver's buildings. That is, to not be there at all – to allow the landscape to remain as intact and pure as possible.

If glass facilitates a certain synthesis of natural and artificial, Vancouver architecture also privileges wood in what can be described as a material semiotics of the natural. A large number of Vancouver buildings feature manufactured wood products. These products play a double role: signifying the forests surrounding the city and indicating increasingly 'sustainable' building construction. Their reconstitution of small wood pieces into larger components both realizes and communicates the increased material efficiency and therefore sustainability of our modes of production. The fact that these components are often deployed in a visually demonstrative and almost ornamental manner reveals the importance of their expressive content in imbuing a building with an emotionally satisfying sustainable naturalism.

Sustainability is the latest variation on nature in the livable city and is fully integrated with supermodel Vancouver. The round of mega-projects that follow Concord Pacific Place and Coal Harbour inflate this aspect of design to a new prominence and scale. This involves incorporating artificially constructed ecological systems directly into buildings and urban space. The Vancouver Convention Centre's green roof and 'bio-engineered' marine habitat are massive ecological investments. The master-planned community at South East False Creek deploys an array of sustainability techniques among its roughly 8,000 units, including the construction of 'Habitat Island'— an artificial island meant to replace lost shoreline while achieving a net increase to inter-tidal fish habitat that supports heightened biodiversity. The leisure oriented nature of the livable city as represented by structures like Coal Harbour's seawall is now expanded to include the non-human residents of the city; residents such as the Great Blue Heron that frequents my condominium tower. Ecological livability is thus the defining double adjective of utopian, supermodel Vancouver.

At the same time that Vancouver is regularly rated as one of world's most livable cities it is also the most murderous large city in Canada, is prohibitively expensive, and the Downtown Eastside includes the most impoverished postal code in the country along with what is reported to be the highest HIV infection rate in the developed world. These are – no doubt – big and serious problems that no urban paradise can claim. But are even the city's utopian aspects so wonderful? Part of the answer is clearly affirmative. That I and thousands of others can live and work in high-density neighborhoods that are defined by light, openness, safety, quiet, and recreational abundance and in which neighborliness extends to wildlife is anathema to the harsh reality of dense settlement for much of human history. But nothing comes without costs and it's interesting to consider just what those costs might be.

To advance this consideration it's useful to think of Vancouver in relation to another even more influential west coast supermodel of utopian urbanism: Disneyland. The livable city and Disneyland have numerous similarities. As the American architect and critic Michael Sorkin reminds us: "Disneyland favors pedestrianism and 'public' transport. It is physically delimited. It is designed to the last detail. It is segmented in 'neighborhoods.'... Its pleasures are all G-rated. It's safe." If Disneyland was built today it would undoubtedly be a model of the most advanced sustainable and ecological design. It's easy to criticize the simulation of the good life that a place like Disneyland represents. Its superficiality and lack of authenticity are obvious. But its example is a useful reminder of the risks inherent in building utopia. Paramount of which, I would argue, are those related to control. Disneyland promises clean safe fun but does so as Sorkin says by offering a "city-like construct that radically circumscribes choice, that heavily polices behavior, that understands subjectivity entirely in terms of consumption and spectatorship, and that sees architecture and space as a territory of fixed and inflexible meanings." It is tempting to see amongst the advantages to utopian Vancouver a resonance with Disneyland's overarching authority that threatens to constrain the expansive and liberating possibilities of the city.

So ask yourself as you explore Vancouver and its architecture: In what ways has the city succeeded in building a benevolent utopia and in what ways has it built its inverse; an attractive and comfortable but ultimately dissatisfying dystopia? Whatever the answer, it is clear that Vancouver's architecture and urbanism is unique. As a relatively young city that at the outset of the 21st Century is still inventing itself, it is exciting to witness so clearly in Vancouver the defining hopes, preoccupations, and struggles to realize the best possible city of the future. More than many other places in the world, Vancouver succinctly manifests this contemporary quest for a new type of city. As an open-ended search it requires both success and failure, but it is the trajectory of the search itself that makes Vancouver such a relevant and fascinating place.

INDEX BY BUILDING TYPE

INDEX BY PROJECT

INDEX BY FIRM

CREDITS

All drawings, renderings and perspectives are reproduced courtesy of the clients, architects, landscape architects, planners and urban designers.

Unless otherwise indicated, the photographs were created by the architects, landscape architects, planners and urban designers or commissioned by each firm. We have made every effort to locate and list the copyright for all illustrations. Where the credit is not listed, it is either held by the architect or we are unable to determine the copyright holder, in which case we would ask that person to contact the publisher.

Photographers' credits:

Peter Aaron, 71 bottom
Tom Arban, 151
Acton Ostry Architects, 38 left, 39
Greg Baluta, 42, 43
Michael Boland, 47 bottom left & right
Busby Perkins+Will, 29 bottom
Cannon Design, 170
Peter Cardew, 84, 85, 129 top
Ricardo Casto, 103 bottom left
James Cheng, 57 bottom right, 59, 71 top & middle
Daniel Collins, 31 bottom right
DA Architects & Planners, 25
Enrico Dagostini, 47 top, 49 bottom right, 155 top & bottom left, 175
Kevin James Day, 57 top
Stan Douglas, 14, 18
James Dow, 31 top, 101, 121, 135
Steve Evans, 122, 123
Shai Gil, 94, 95
Raef Grohne, 60, 61
Henriquez Partners, 41 bottom right
Ivan Hunter, 109
Timothy Hursley, 129 bottom
Stephen Hynes, 103 top
Hubert Kang, 138, 139 bottom, 171 bottom left

Alan Kaplanas, 106
Lori Kiessling & Pax Lyle, 183
Gerry Kopelow, 31 bottom left, 102, 125 top & bottom left
Mike Laanela, 81
Nic Lehoux, 29, 38 right, 67, 74, 75, 78, 79, 93, 97, 115, 119, 139 top, 142, 143, 155 middle left, middle right, bottom right, 158, 159, 160, 161, 164, 165, 171 top & bottom right, 177
Derek Leper, 22, 23, 40, 41 top & bottom left, 45 bottom, 54, 55, 168, 169
Gavin Mackenzie, cover, 2, 8, 53 bottom left, 145 top, 178
Bob Matheson, 37, 53 bottom right, 57 bottom left, 96, 107 top
Heather Maxwell, 125 bottom right
Nicole Milkovich, 103 bottom right
Gary Otte, 88, 89
Bill Pechet, 32, 33, 145 bottom left & right, 148, 149
Tony Robbins, 107 bottom
Salt Tasting Room, 48, 49 top & bottom left
Simon Scott, 111 bottom right
Danny Singer, 27, 73 top
Martin Tessler, 64, 65, 126, 127, 130, 131, 173
Horst Thanhauser, 108
Peter Timmermans, 66

Neighbourhoods in the guidebook